Our Incoming
WORLD GOVERNMENT
~God's Kingdom

A Look Just Ahead Under the Brightening Light of Bible Prophecies That Are Nearing Fulfillment in the One Form of Rulership That Will Satisfy All Our Needs and Desires

"God is King of all the earth; make melody, acting with discretion. God has become king over the nations. God himself has taken his seat upon his holy throne."
—Psalm 47:7, 8.

DEDICATED to the God whose happy time has come to replace man's disastrous rulership of himself with the righteous government for which heartsick people of all races have longed.

Publishers
WATCHTOWER BIBLE AND TRACT SOCIETY
OF NEW YORK, INC.
INTERNATIONAL BIBLE STUDENTS ASSOCIATION
BROOKLYN, NEW YORK, U.S.A.

FIRST EDITION
2,000,000 Copies

Made in the United States of America

CONTENTS

Unless otherwise indicated, all quotations and citations made in this book are taken from the *New World Translation of the Holy Scriptures* (*NW*), 1971 edition.

In connection with dates, the abbreviation B.C.E. stands for "Before the Common Era," and C.E. stands for "Of the Common Era."

EGYPT

ASSYRIA

BABYLON

ROME

GREECE

MEDO-PERSIA

BRITAIN-AMERICA

UNITED NATIONS

GOD'S KINGDOM

CHAPTER 1

The Next Rulership
for All the Earth

L OVERS of righteous rulership are thrilled at the mere thought of it. The day of the long-promised world government is dawning. Within our favored generation that government will rise like the sun in a cloudless sky to flood the earth with its welcome light, ushering in a time of radiant living for all mankind. What is brought to light should delight our eyes.

² A transformed scene brightens before our eyes. Human relations were once so difficult. But look! What happens under the greatly needed world government when in control? Everywhere the oneness of the human family is acknowledged and abided by in all honesty and happiness. Everyone is a friend to everybody else. The bonds of family relationship are felt to the depths of each one's soul. Along with this enjoyable fellowship, there is a fine spirit of helpfulness with sincere interest in the others' welfare. Divisive racism is no longer rampant. All make up one human race, with common blood ties, all being of one origin.

³ Listen! All the subjects of the world government are understanding one another. They are

1. Lovers of righteous rulership are thrilled at the thought of what? Why?
2. What delights our eyes about the state of human relationships?
3. Why is it that they all understand one another when speaking?

5

speaking a common world language! Why, that is like going back to the original speech pattern of the human family! Back until some forty-one centuries ago all humans spoke the same language. All men had the one vocabulary, making it possible for them to understand one another's speech. This made it easy for them to work together in any common project. Then, suddenly, there came a confusion of language. Many languages sprang up! Local dialects developed. O what division this brought! National languages became a treasure jealously guarded and insisted upon for preservation. This is something that only the world government can deal with successfully. It will!

⁴ The world government takes away all language barriers between its subjects. National pride of language is wiped out. National distinctions are gone! No one is a citizen of this or that nation. All are world citizens, yes, citizens of one new world. The one language that they all speak for mutual understanding is the language recognized and used by the world government, the official language. It is mankind's original language, which everybody on earth spoke for the first eighteen hundred years of human existence. That original language was developed to a high degree and it never did really die out, for a small minority of people persisted in its use, also the greatest book on earth preserving it.

⁵ Oneness of language makes it easier for traveling abroad. Does a person's occupation or profession call for him to do some traveling to parts of the earth distant from his home? How won-

---

4. Of what are they citizens, and what is their language?
5. What changes are there for those who must travel far from home?

derful it is, how easygoing it is for him to have no further need of a passport! He does not need to have a health certificate; he does not have to cross international borders and go through immigration checkpoints and through customs inspection. There is no tax on imports. There are no money exchange rates to worry about and to figure out, there being no different currencies in use in the territories formerly under national rulerships. For a person to escape going through entrance or exit formalities along with visas of permission, he would formerly have had to get off the earth. But who wants to do this? However, world government brings a change on that score.

⁶ Surely, though, there must be different laws and ordinances for the different localities on earth. No, not at all! That used to be the case when there were city, county, state or provincial and national lawmaking bodies. At that time the public sale and drinking of alcoholic beverages were unlawful in one county, but in the adjoining county there was no prohibition. In one country the importation of certain harmful drugs was strictly forbidden, but in another the growing of plants and the production of harmful drugs and the sale and exportation of such drugs were legal operations and brought financial income to the government that legalized such. In one land dominated by a certain religious faith it was perfectly all right for a man to have two or more wives, but in another land a man could be brought into the law courts and punished for being merely a bigamist. Laws differed from country to country, and the legal profession, the lawyers, the bar-

6. What about world government and conflicting laws here and there?

risters, the legal consultants abounded. But now in the new order under world government, there is but the one set of laws for all the earth.

7 Another thing is also very noticeable under the new world government. The general health of the people appears to be getting better all the time. There is no mistaking this. The health of the obedient subjects of the world government is really improving. Why, aches and pains are vanishing, wrinkles are disappearing from once worried or timeworn faces. Even those bent over from weakness and old age are gradually straightening up and walking with graceful erectness. All around us there are signs that the persons of advanced years are returning to the days of their youth. Evidently, everyone is enjoying the privilege of living, and each new day is greeted with thankfulness for the added day of life. Bodily infirmity is not increasing as time goes on. Physical forces are building up, and the bodies are not wearing out. Whatever the "medicine" it is that the world government is administering, its medical aid is producing wonders. It will finally bring human perfection.

8 Even mankind's natural environment is getting better and better. All nature is being rejuvenated. The whole earth is becoming one global beauty spot. The world government has an expert weather bureau that is never wrong. It really has complete weather control. From no part of the earth is there any report of drought or rainfall in ruinous downpours, or cyclones, hurricanes, typhoons. All the forces of nature are being brought into a

7. What is to be said about the "medicine" then administered?
8. Earth's changing appearance shows what about weather control?

perfect balance for making the whole earth an exquisite place in which to live. There is no lack of food anywhere, for the earth is yielding its products to the full. Human needs in the way of food are being amply met, and all of this is contributing to the improving health of the people. Freedom from fear of want prevails. The spirit of neighborliness moves all to liberality, to mutual helpfulness and sharing. All speaking the one language, all feeling the close bonds of family relationship, all being fellow citizens subject to the world government, all are joining together in making their earthly home as beautiful a place as possible in which to live together forever.

PERFECT HEALTH FOR ENJOYING LIFE

⁹ In order to bring an equality to all its subjects for the physical enjoyment of living, the world government engages in a repair work of the bodies and minds of all its loyal subjects. Who is there of us that does not have something wrong with him? As respects body and mind, some are worse off than others. Think of those who have lost one or more limbs of the body. Think of those who have their limbs but who through paralysis derive no pleasure from the use of them. Think of those whose internal organs have been impaired so that their bodies do not function normally. The world government's take-over of the full management of human affairs may find individuals still afflicted with hideous diseases. Some have eyes that do not literally see, others have ears but live in a soundless realm, others have the organs of speech but cannot use them to com-

9. What bodily inequalities will exist at first as to one's enjoying life?

municate with others who can hear articulate speech. Imagine all the bodily inequalities that are bound to exist at first with regard to everyone's sharing fully in all the joys and blessings of living under the established world government!

¹⁰ How ably this new rulership proves itself equal to the needs of the situation! What a grand contribution it makes to the human perfection that works for perfect living by *all* its devoted subjects! The lame walk, yes, skip around for joy. Lost arms and legs are miraculously restored. The blind see, the deaf hear, the dumb speak and sing for sheer joy. Unsightliness about human form and figure disappears. For personal appearance it is a generation of mankind of which the government can rightly be proud. What wonder, then, that there are no hospitals to be found, no insane asylums, no quarantined colonies where persons afflicted with dread contagious diseases are isolated!

¹¹ Ah, indeed, life will be worth living then! But why should a generation of mankind that merely happened to be living at a certain time in human history be so favored with the precious opportunity of living in human perfection in a perfect earthly environment? What about the previous generations? What about near relatives who have died of natural causes or other circumstances, yes, the ancestors of all these living subjects of the world government? They yet live in the memories of these living sharers in the blessings of the righteous new order. No less so the world government has in mind those who have

---

10. How is ability to meet the health needs of all demonstrated?
11. How did time favor the generation thus enjoying such things?

returned to the dust of the ground from which the first man was originally taken.

[12] The world government does not need any tombstones, mausoleums or other grave markers to remind it of those who were relentlessly claimed by mankind's common enemy, Death. It is a government for the benefit of not just the living subjects, but also the countless human dead, compared with which the yet living ones are but a small fraction. It has grand purposes for the dead also. It has instilled in the hearts of the living the hope of welcoming back to life under the world government those who sleep the sleep of death in the dust of the ground. It stands ready to give instructions to its living subjects to make warm, loving preparations and provisions for the return of the dead. The world government wants the whole earth comfortably filled with subjects, and the resurrection of the human dead is the main way for carrying out this marvelous government project. In view of its superhuman power, no problem is posed for it by such a thing as the resurrection of all the victims of death.

[13] What, though, of all the religious beliefs, ideas and tendencies that the resurrected ones will bring back with them? During their former lifetime on earth, religion had been the most divisive force plaguing mankind. Because of the religious background of the resurrected ones, will not their restoration to life result in a terribly divided world, reviving religious prejudices, hatreds and hostilities of a violent kind?

---

12. How will the world government show itself aware of the dead?
13. What question about religion does the resurrection stir up?

¹⁴ Well, as we look at the earthly scene under the world government, we ask ourselves: 'Where are the steepled or highly domed religious structures, cathedrals, basilicas, mosques, shrines, the imposing religious images and statues?' They are gone! Members of today's generation that are still alive are getting along in unity without all those religious adjuncts. Their form of worship conforms to actual truth. Their faith and practice are what the world government approves of, for these are free of all man-made fables, myths and fanciful legends and fraud. As for the resurrected dead, O how they will be disillusioned, especially those who at death expected to find themselves as angels in heaven or as conscious souls in the flames of a purgatory or hell of eternal torment, or undergoing a transmigration or in a state of Nirvana! Resurrection to life on earth will certainly be a mighty corrective to their religious thinking and understanding.

¹⁵ The resurrected ones will learn that the world government is one of truth, tolerating no religious error. So, they will now be taught the truth and nothing but the truth. Unitedly the whole human race will be able to worship with truth as well as in all sincerity.

¹⁶ We have already taken note of the absence of buildings of the former kind that were devoted to religion out of line with truth. So, too, now we see no men and women going around dressed in queer garb like a priestly or clergy class, demanding special treatment and favors and rev-

---

14. Why will resurrection correct religious thinking of persons raised from the dead?
15. How will resurrected ones be enabled to worship correctly?
16. Why do we see none parading around like priests or clergymen?

erence. Those who are resurrected from the dead will not be restored to their former religious stations, with a renewal of religious confusion and strife. Gone are their privileged positions that exalted them over the common people for whom they officiated in palatial religious edifices. Salvation of the ordinary man, woman and child used to be considered dependent upon the services of such dignitaries. But now the world government is charged with caring for the eternal salvation of its earthly subjects in perfect health and happiness upon a Paradise earth. The government's ability to remove bodily infirmities and even raise the dead to life proves that fact. It is human nature to worship something, and the world government is filling that need by teaching its subjects the pure worship that is life sustaining.

LOCATION OF WORLD GOVERNMENT

[17] By now we may be wondering, Where on earth is the capital city of this world government? Look where we will on earth, we do not locate it. It has to be somewhere. Yes, but not here on earth. And reasonably so! A world government that can do such grand things of lasting benefit to its subjects certainly ranks higher than any type of human government that has ever ruled on earth. This comparison holds true even in our age of modern science, technology, advanced medicine, mechanized farming and nuclear power. A world government that has to its credit all the marvelous accomplishments discussed earlier displays that it has superhuman power, yes, supernatural abilities. It proves itself to be more than a man-made government. Here on earth, among

17. Despite its location, how does the government prove real?

men, is therefore not the place to look for its location. Its location must be higher than on earth. It must be above us, up in heaven. That is why it is invisible to us here on earth. But by all the good it does to its earthly subjects, it demonstrates itself to be real, existing!

[18] The fact that the world government is so highly elevated above its earthly subjects serves to increase man's respect for it. Its rulings are taken more seriously by earthling man. The rightfulness of its sovereignty over all the earth is appreciated, hence submitted to in a humble way. Its wisdom is seen to be far superior to that of any earthly rulership in human history. It has unselfish interest in its earthly subjects. So its running of human affairs is better than that by any earthly government during the preceding six millenniums of man's history.

[19] Well, then, should it seem strange that the world government is heavenly? No; for we should bear in mind that man is not the monarch of all he surveys. Man's planet Earth is not the center of the universe, but its invisible heavenly Maker is. As a planet, it revolves around a visible center, namely, the sun, some ninety-three million miles away. Our earth and its sun are part of the Milky Way and, as such, they are slowly revolving around the axis of this same magnificent galaxy made up of billions of brilliant suns. Necessarily, then, we who live on earth find ourselves also revolving around the heavenly Maker of our earth, of our solar system, of our Milky Way galaxy, yes,

18. Its being heavenly has what effect on its subjects?
19. (a) Why are we earthlings revolving around the Creator of the universe? (b) Why can he set up a world government for us?

of all galaxies that are known to modern astronomers by means of the most powerful telescopes. Even in a physical sense we inhabiters of tiny Earth are controlled, governed by physical laws of the universe. Why should anyone question, then, that the Maker of all those physical laws that keep the enormous universe in such awe-inspiring harmony and unity is able to set up a perfect government for all the world of mankind?

²⁰ Unless the next rulership for all the earth were the world government established by the Maker of all the heavenly galaxies and of us on earth, the human family would be doomed to eternal extinction. The next rulership for all the earth needs to be, indeed it has to be, that of the Creator of all the universe, or else all is lost for us. How glad we can be that it will prove to be the long-promised Government issuing from Him! Every government ever in existence has had a purpose for its being set up and operating. The incoming world government, too, has a purpose, the most glorious of all purposes. First of all, it will prove to man on earth that there is an intelligent, all-wise, all-powerful, all-just, perfectly loving God, the Creator and Sovereign of all the universe. The proof of that, the verification of that, is of first importance, for all things everywhere, living and lifeless, seen and unseen, depend upon Him; they exist and are maintained by Him.

²¹ The secondary purpose of this incoming world government is the rescue of the human race from the final outcome of all wrongdoing, namely, death, yes, endless destruction. Not that we puny

---

20. (a) Why is it needful for man's next rulership to be that world government? (b) What is its primary purpose?
21. What is the secondary purpose of this government, and why?

humans are so important to God, not that he could not get along without us on earth. He could easily do so, but he does not want to do so. Why? All because he loves all of us as his creatures, the work of his hands, and he made us to be perfectly happy in him as our heavenly Father and to be an honor to him.

[22] Should that not make us want God's world government to be the next rulership for all the earth? All of us whose hearts are not hardened and embittered by all the badness of fallen human society should be warmed at heart to the point of saying Yes! We whose hearts are still sensitive to undeserved expressions of divine love will be keenly interested in knowing what assurances from Him we have for expecting him to bring in this righteous world government. Why, also, will He do this within our own generation? Most certain it is that our taking in this knowledge of Him and his greathearted purpose will contribute to our gaining life everlasting in blessed relationship with the incoming world government.

---

22. So, what are we interested in knowing, with what benefit?

CHAPTER 2

The Governor Who Knows the End from the Beginning

THROUGHOUT all the ages from the days of ancient Babylon till now, political rulers have consulted astrologers and clairvoyants or spirit mediums to find out what the future holds. They have sought supernatural foreknowledge to aid them in governing their peoples with success. Political history down till into the last quarter of the twentieth century proves that all information thus gained has failed them. So the state of worldly politics is a mess. The governors of human affairs do not know which way to turn. The nations are in anguish and are resorting to high-handed measures, and the people have every reason to fear the worst. For a real remedy they can turn to no one on earth. The only successful direction in which to turn is away from astrologers, spirit mediums and the occult source of their misleading information and look up to the Supreme Governor of all things, the Most High God from whom the incoming world government comes!

[2] No historian, no well-informed person, can deny that from the earliest times the nations of the world have had their gods, visible and invisible. Why, shortly after the end of World

---

1. Unlike politicians, where must we look to know of the future?
2. Proof of godship rests upon what ability as to prophecy?

War II in 1945 the emperor of Japan renounced the claim that he was a god, the descendant of the Japanese sun-goddess Amaterasu, and yet, to this day, many traditional religionists hold on to emperor worship in the Land of the Rising Sun. These so-called "gods" of the nations have had their prophets on earth. For instance, in the tenth century before our Common Era, the prophets of the god Baal numbered four hundred and fifty in the Middle Eastern nation of Israel, during the reign of King Ahab and Queen Jezebel, as reported in the book of 1 Kings, chapter eighteen, verse twenty-two. Such prophets made predictions of the future in the name of their god. If the prophecy made in the name of a god did not come true, it proved the god to be false, a no-god. In fact, the proof of a true god rested upon his ability to fulfill his prophecy!

³ Under this crucial test of prophecy, who is it that proved to be the real God, the living and true God? The prophets of the gods of the nations stood as witnesses to produce the facts about their gods and to point to the prophecies that their gods had made come true. Have any of these national gods made prophecies that are of value today, that are coming true in our modern times? Can anybody, can any historical authority, offer as evidence one such prophecy? Nobody today can do so! And yet there is one God that offers himself as willing to submit to the test of prophecy, to prove that he is the one living and true God who has foreknowledge and can foretell the future and whose prophecies have all along come true. He can produce his witnesses with

3. Prophets should be witnesses for their gods in what respect?

historical proof in support of his being a God of true prophecy. Who is He? What is His name?

⁴ One of his prophets who lived in the eighth century before our Common Era was Isaiah the son of Amoz, a subject of the Middle Eastern kingdom of Judah. The spirit of inspiration came upon him and he was thus used as a mouthpiece to issue the following challenge to all the gods of the nations, saying:

⁵ "Let the nations all be collected together at one place, and let national groups be gathered together. Who is there among them [the gods of the nations and peoples] that can tell this? Or can they cause us to hear even the first things? Let them [as gods] furnish their witnesses, that they [as gods] may be declared righteous, or let them [the nations and national groups] hear and say, 'It is the truth!' "—Isaiah 43:9.

⁶ In those words, the gods of the nations and of the <u>national groups are challenged as to their prophetic powers.</u> Who among such national gods is able to declare prophetically what has been foretold in the preceding verses of this chapter of Isaiah's prophecy? Who among those national gods can cause us to hear in advance the very first things that are to happen in the immediate future, not to speak of the final things of the future?

⁷ <u>Let these national gods furnish their witnesses on earth</u> to testify that these gods have done these things of a prophetic kind with accuracy,

4-6. What challenge does Isaiah 43:9 pose to the national gods?
7. Who should serve as their witnesses and who should hear them?

so as to prove by these witnesses that they are true, reliable gods and deserve to be declared right, righteous, fully justified in being worshiped as gods with ability to forecast the future unfailingly. Or, let the gathered nations and national groups hear such witnesses of the gods and pass upon the testimony of those witnesses and say that what they are testifying is correct, is truth, is historical fact. The challenged national gods have proved unable to produce such witnesses. There are no witnesses of theirs of whose testimony we can say: "It is the truth!"

[8] And now comes the declaration of the challenger: According to the American Standard Version (*AS*) of the Bible, the challenger identifies who he is by name, saying: "<u>Ye are my witnesses, saith Jehovah,</u> and my servant whom I have chosen; that ye may know and believe me, and understand that I am he: before me there was no God formed, neither shall there be after me. I, even I, am Jehovah; and besides me there is no saviour. I have declared, and I have saved, and I have showed; and there was no strange *god* among you: therefore ye are my witnesses, saith Jehovah, and I am God. Yea, since the day was I am he; and there is none that can deliver out of my hand: I will work, and who can hinder it?"—Isaiah 43:10-13; see also the *New World Translation of the Holy Scriptures.*

[9] Boldly the One who raised the challenging questions identifies himself as Jehovah. Whereas the challenged gods cannot produce their witnesses to furnish evidence of their godship, Je-

8. Who does the challenger identify himself to be?
9. Whom has Jehovah made his witnesses, and how?

hovah can produce His witnesses. His witnesses are on the scene. He has furnished them, and he addresses them and reminds them of how they came to be His witnesses. Who are they? <u>Jehovah speaks of them as a unit, calling them as a group,</u> "My servant whom I have chosen." They stand in contrast with the nations and national groups whose many gods Jehovah challenges. <u>Jehovah's witnesses are his own servant, his own chosen nation.</u> That this nation might be his unanimous witnesses, <u>Jehovah has made it his servant class that they might get acquainted with him:</u> that they might know him and believe, have faith, in him, and hence understand that he is the same One, the unchanged, everlasting God. In this way they could be equipped to serve as his witnesses before all the idolatrous nations of the world.

[10] Before this God, Jehovah, there was no such person or thing as a god formed. Not that Jehovah God himself was formed by someone. If, like modern atheists, we were to insist that Jehovah God was formed, we should be obliged logically to ask, Who formed Jehovah God? This would lead to the question, Who, then, formed the former of Jehovah God? Also, Who formed the one that formed the former of Jehovah God? In fact, we should never get to the end of asking that same question over and over again. Thus the mystery about Godship would only thicken, get more complicated and lead to no satisfaction of an intelligent mind. The question of formation could only cease to be asked when it reached an un-

---

10. How is it that there was no god formed before Jehovah?

formed Former who had always been, a Former without beginning. The prophet Moses, who was one of the witnesses that made up Jehovah's "servant" class, settles the matter in a most simple timesaving way, saying to the Lord Jehovah, the Creator of heaven and earth: <u>"Even from everlasting to everlasting, thou art God."</u>—Psalm 90:1, 2, *AS*.

¹¹ Why, then, did Jehovah say: "Before me there was no God formed"? (Isaiah 43:10) It was because <u>the idolatrous nations of the world had formed their own false gods, but they had not formed Jehovah as God</u>. They were not ahead of Jehovah's existence in forming a single false god of theirs. Jehovah, as the Creator of the earth and its inhabitants, was ahead of any and all the nations. For that reason, there was no god formed by the idolatrous nations before Jehovah.

¹² Not only that, but, says Jehovah, "neither shall there be after me." (*AS*) Jehovah being God "even from everlasting to everlasting," he will never pass off the scene. <u>The idolatrous nations</u>, not being everlasting, will <u>pass off the earthly scene</u> during the world's greatest trouble just ahead, <u>whereas the everlasting Jehovah will survive to everlasting</u>. So, the nations will not be here after Jehovah, but He after them. Hence, it is impossible for the idolatrous nations to continue forming their false gods after Jehovah. Their formed or man-made gods will perish with them. (Isaiah 2:18-21) But Jehovah the true God of prophecy lives on everlastingly. Also, his faithful witnesses will live on eternally, ever on hand to

11. Why is it that there was no god formed before Jehovah?
12. Why will there be no god formed after Jehovah?

testify vocally in support of the Godship of Jehovah.

[13] Many of the ancient nations, Babylon, Assyria, Medo-Persia, Edom (Idumea), Moab, Ammon and others, have long since been out of existence, and their manufactured gods passed away with them. As regards those national gods, Jehovah God can say: "After me there continued to be none. I— I am Jehovah, and besides me there is no savior." —Isaiah 43:10, 11, *NW*.

THE CREATING OF WITNESSES

[14] To have witnesses, this beginningless God who had no one that formed him would have to do, say or prophesy something, and this before observers or in front of those who benefit therefrom. He did create witnesses by doing something for them, so that they could truthfully say something about him. In fact, he saved these witnesses, as he had told forth that he would do. And this he did without the assistance of any so-called "god." In this way he visibly demonstrated that he was God, the only living and true God. This is what he went on to call to our attention in the further words of the prophet Isaiah:

[15] " 'I myself have told forth and have saved and have caused it to be heard, when there was among you no strange god. So you are my witnesses,' is the utterance of Jehovah, 'and I am God. Also, all the time I am the same One; and there is no one effecting deliverance out of my own hand. I shall get active, and who can turn it [my action] back?' "—Isaiah 43:12, 13, *NW*.

---

13. In what cases have no gods continued to be after Jehovah?
14, 15. How did Jehovah create his witnesses, doing so unaided?

[16] The saved ones were unable to attribute their salvation to anyone else but the One who had said beforehand that he would do it. His act of salvation he caused to be heard abroad. So his saved ones were under obligation to be his witnesses, in order to verify what others had merely heard about. He had proved himself to be God, and so he was not a god without valid witnesses to this truth.

[17] Furthermore, he was God Almighty, for nobody could deliver himself or deliver anyone else out of Jehovah's hand. When Jehovah takes action, nobody is able to turn it back or reverse it. What he foretells or prophesies, he is powerful enough to make come true.

[18] Jehovah saved his "servant" class of witnesses once before, in 1513 B.C.E., and he can do it again, even on a grander scale. He had saved Israel from the Egyptian Empire, when it was a world power, the First World Power on Bible record. Even the later Babylonian Empire, the Third World Power in Bible history, would not be strong enough to block a second salvation of Jehovah's servant. Looking ahead to such a salvation in the sixth century before our Common Era, the Almighty God went on to say by his prophet Isaiah two centuries ahead of time: "This is what Jehovah has said, the Repurchaser of you people, the Holy One of Israel: 'For your sakes I will send to Babylon and cause the bars of the prisons to come down, and the Chaldeans in the ships with whining cries on their part. I am Jehovah your Holy One,

---

16. To whom were the saved ones obliged to attribute salvation?
17. When He takes action, why can nobody else turn it back?
18. How did Jehovah repeat salvation, but on a grander scale?

the Creator of Israel, your King.'"—Isaiah 43:14, 15.

[19] Thus, as if the salvation of his captive people Israel had already occurred, the God who was responsible for the creation of that nation speaks of himself as its Repurchaser, its Redeemer from the Babylonian World Power. For their sakes he would send the combined military forces of the Medes and the Persians, under Cyrus the Great, to overthrow the Babylonian Empire in the year 539 B.C.E. All the ships of Babylon on the Euphrates River, whether military or commercial, would not be able to halt Babylon's downfall. In place of shouts of triumph, the seamen would give way to whining cries. Why should this not be the case as their ships got stranded when the military strategist Cyrus caused the waters of the Euphrates River to be turned aside from their regular channel in order for his troops to slosh their way down the riverbed and thus gain entrance to the city through the waterfront gates?

[20] Ancient Babylon as a political world power had refused to open her prison system by which she held the deported Israelites in exile, isolated a thousand miles from their desolated homeland, Jerusalem and the land of the kingdom of Judah. But, in carrying out his foretold role according to the prophecy of Isaiah (44:28–45:4), Cyrus the conqueror was moved to act to break the prison bars and let liberty-loving Israelite exiles return to their desolated country in 537 B.C.E. Jehovah God, the Fulfiller of prophecy, let his

19. How did the Repurchaser Jehovah make Chaldean seamen whine?
20. For whom did Cyrus the Great break the prison bars, and how?

debt to the Emancipator Cyrus be charged to His account. As Israel's Repurchaser he duly rewarded Cyrus.—Isaiah 43:3, 4.

²¹ At the heartbreaking destruction of Jerusalem and its temple by the Babylonians in 607 B.C.E., Israelite kings ceased to sit on "Jehovah's throne" at that capital city. (1 Chronicles 29:23) But now, by his deliverance of his exiled people from Babylon in 537 B.C.E., Jehovah God proved that he was still their heavenly King. (Isaiah 52:7; Matthew 5:35) Their God, not some human creature, was their King. They were, first of all, *His* subjects. They owed their loyalty to Him, even as they owed their release from Babylon to Him, and not to his earthly agent, Cyrus the Persian. He had foretold his repurchase of them from the prison-keeper Babylon, and he could never break his given word. So, now, not only their ancient forefathers, but they themselves also were His witnesses.

²² If all of this did not prove that He was the one living and true God, what more could be required of him? From first to last, from all times past to all times future, he alone holds the field of Godship. Witnesses on earth to his Godship are not lacking. Confidently from his supreme position of Godship, he can make his further challenging declaration before the gods of all nations:

²³ "This is what Jehovah has said, the King of Israel and the Repurchaser of him, Jehovah of armies, 'I am the first and I am the last, and be-

sides me there is no God. And who is there like me? Let him call out, that he may tell it and present it to me. From when I appointed the people of long ago, both the things coming and the things that will enter in let them [these gods] tell on their part. Do not be in dread, you people, and do not become stupefied. Have I not from that time on caused you individually to hear and told it out? And you are my witnesses. Does there exist a God besides me? No, there is no Rock. I have recognized none.' "—Isaiah 44:6-8.

²⁴ How do we today feel about this matter? Would any of us feel honored if the God of the Holy Bible, Jehovah, were to say to us: "You are my witnesses"? We would have reason to feel honored, for this would place us in a highly honored class.

²⁵ The prophet Isaiah himself was one of Jehovah's witnesses, was he not? Certainly the prophetic book of Isaiah, sixty-six chapters in length, and the many quotations from it as found in the inspired Christian Scriptures, from Matthew to Revelation, all prove that Isaiah was outstanding as a witness of Jehovah. And what about Jesus Christ himself? Can anyone in heaven or on earth deny that he, too, was a witness of Jehovah? Nobody anywhere and of any time outranks him as such a witness. As a born Jew or Israelite, Jesus Christ was part of that nation to whom the words of Isaiah 43:10 were addressed: " 'You are my witnesses,' is the utterance of Jehovah, 'even my servant whom I have chosen.' " If no other man does so, the apostle John

---

24, 25. Why is it an honor to be addressed as His witnesses?

calls him "Jesus Christ, 'the Faithful Witness.'" And John also quotes the resurrected Jesus as saying: "These are the things that the Amen says, the faithful and true witness, the beginning of the creation by God."—Revelation 1:5; 3:14.

MODERN-DAY WITNESSES OF JEHOVAH

[26] Since Jesus Christ was and confessed to be Jehovah's witness, is it at all out of order that faithful disciples of Christ today should recognize themselves as Jehovah's witnesses and confess to being such? Of course not! These faithful imitators of Jesus Christ endeavor to live up to their profession of being Jehovah's witnesses by bearing witness to Him and His kingdom world wide, in compliance with Jesus' words of prophecy at Matthew 24:14. Jehovah, whose witnesses they are, is the Being whom they worship as the one living and true God. They recognize Him as the One who delivered them from a politico-religious organization more powerful than ancient Babylon on the Euphrates River, namely, from what the last book of the Bible calls Babylon the Great.

[27] Many Bible students have thought that Babylon the Great symbolized the Roman Catholic Church with its capital at the seven-hilled city of Rome. Others have thought her to symbolize bloodstained Christendom with its babel of religious sects. But the Bible identifies Babylon the Great as the world empire of false religion, Christendom included.—Revelation 14:8; 17:3 through 18:4.

26, 27. (a) Why should real Christians also be Jehovah's witnesses? (b) From what imperial organization has he delivered them?

[28] The Bible Christianity, not Christendom, stands absolutely separate and distinct from Babylon the Great. There are true Christians today who can bear witness to Jehovah as having delivered them from the religious world empire of Babylon the Great. They know from the Bible prophecies that Jehovah foretold this modern-day deliverance, even as he also foreshadowed it by delivering the repentant remnant of Israelites from ancient Babylon in 537 B.C.E. They know that to deliver them Jehovah has used someone mightier than ancient Cyrus the Great, who came from the east of Babylon to overthrow her as a world power. Jehovah used as the deliverer of His modern-day witnesses the one whom He anointed with His holy spirit at his baptism in the Jordan River, Jesus Christ. This anointed one is the antitypical Cyrus, and he speeds like an eagle to the act of delivering Jehovah's modern witnesses from Babylon the Great. The liberated witnesses are grateful to Jehovah for calling this Greater Cyrus to swoop down like a bird of prey upon Babylon the Great and free them from her religious prison.

[29] The faith of these delivered witnesses in Jehovah as God has been strengthened. In themselves they know for a fact that he foretold their deliverance long ago and that he has actually brought it about. It is faith strengthening to them to know that the counsel that he long ago took with himself to carry out he has indeed followed to brilliant success today. Ask them, and they

---

28. Who is the Greater Cyrus, and how has he been like an eagle?
29, 30. What can Jehovah's witnesses testify as to His counsel?

will bear witness as to how true their God has proved to be to his prophetic declaration in Isaiah 46:8-11, where we read:

[30] "Remember this, that you people may muster up courage. Lay it to heart, you transgressors. Remember the first things of a long time ago, that I am the Divine One and there is no other God, nor anyone like me; the One telling from the beginning the finale, and from long ago the things that have not been done; the One saying, 'My own counsel will stand, and everything that is my delight I shall do'; the One calling from the sunrising a bird of prey, from a distant land the man to execute my counsel. I have even spoken it; I shall also bring it in. I have formed it, I shall also do it."—*NW;* see also The Jewish Publication Society of America Bible.

THE ONE WHO KNOWS THE END
FROM THE BEGINNING

[31] This is the kind of undefeatable God that all the nations of the earth have to deal with today. Because he is the God of infallible counsel, he is the Divine One "telling from the beginning the finale, and from long ago the things that have not been done." (Isaiah 46:10) It is high time that the earthly nations took this God Jehovah seriously and considered his purposeful counsel that stands plainly written in the Holy Bible. He is able to take on as an opponent any world power that exists today, no matter how mightily armed with nuclear weapons it may be. In the sixth century B.C.E. he took on the Babylonian World Power, which was mercilessly oppressing his wit-

---

31, 32. How did Jehovah hold to his counsel against Assyria?

nesses. Before that he took on another attacker of his witnesses, namely, the Assyrian World Power, and sent what was left of its invading armies reeling back to its capital city Nineveh in military disgrace. In the words recorded in Isaiah 14:24-27, he foretold what he would do to warlike Assyria, saying:

[32] "Jehovah of armies has sworn, saying: 'Surely just as I have figured, so it must occur; and just as I have counseled, that is what will come true, in order to break the Assyrian in my land and that I may tread him down on my own mountains; and that his yoke may actually depart from upon them and that his very load may depart from upon their shoulder.' This is the counsel that is counseled against all the earth, and this is the hand that is stretched out against all the nations. For Jehovah of armies himself has counseled, and who can break it up? And his hand is the one stretched out, and who can turn it back?"

[33] Today, more than 2,700 years later, it is our right and privilege to ask, Did things occur just as Jehovah had thought and come true just as he had counseled with himself? Did Jehovah of armies break the Assyrian invader in Jehovah's own Promised Land and tread him down in the mountains of that land? For an answer, all we have to do is to turn back to that night in the year 732 B.C.E. King Sennacherib's delegation had served his final proposition upon Jerusalem. Jehovah by his prophet Isaiah then sent his own derisive reply back to Sennacherib, who was then besieging Libnah, about twenty miles (32 kilo-

---

33, 34. How did Jehovah's executing his counsel affect Sennacherib?

meters) westward from Jerusalem. Then one hundred and eighty-five thousand of Sennacherib's warriors retired for the night to sink into so sound a sleep that they never woke up. With a silent death-dealing blow Jehovah's angel struck them.

34 On arising in the morning, boastful Sennacherib must have been terrified at the sight of his military camp. Crushed, he finally realized that he could not contend with success against such a God as Jehovah. So with what troops survived that horrendous night he scurried out of the land of Judah and back to the Assyrian capital, Nineveh. If Jehovah could do such a slaughter to Sennacherib's troops at a distance of twenty or more miles from Jerusalem, what could this God do to the Assyrian army at close range in a siege right at Jerusalem? It was too horrifying for Sennacherib to think about. He never tried to threaten the city of the Great King Jehovah again.—Isaiah 36:1 through 37:38; 2 Chronicles 32:20-22.

35 Here in this actual happening of ancient history there is plenty of food for thought on the part of the modern Anglo-American World Power, yes, on the part of the Communist bloc of nations, also on the part of all the nations of today no matter of what sort of political complexion they may be. They are dealing with the same God as the One who carried out his own counsel toward King Sennacherib the ruler of the Assyrian World Power, which dominated the world during the eighth and seventh centuries B.C.E. This same God, Jehovah, has made known his thoughts concerning all the nations now acting on this

35. For executing what counsel is his hand now stretched out?

twentieth-century world stage, and what he has thought concerning them is what we of this generation are certain to see occur in our time. His own private counsel he has revealed to us. We find it recorded on the pages of the Bible, and who is there on earth today that has the ability to break up His counsel? His almighty hand is now being stretched out for the execution of his judicial counsel, and not even all the nations combined can turn his hand back and ward off destruction.

HIS GOOD PROMISES SURE

[36] Today mankind is faced with destruction by a nuclear Third World War and the ruination of man's natural environment. So what about Jehovah's counsel concerning a world government? From the very time that man went wrong and set out on a course of self-government independent of his heavenly Father, Jehovah God has thought about a world government as the only solution to mankind's increasing troubles and problems. He immediately counseled in favor of such a global government, with himself as the Supreme Governor. His thought and counsel are not vain ideas of his mind. He knows exactly how to bring what he has thought and counseled to reality. He knows how his thought and counsel will be worked out, and he knows what the end will be. He has all the power and dynamic energy by means of which to reach that glorious end. Hence he is "the One telling from the beginning the finale." He is the Governor who knows the end

---

36. Why are His thought and counsel on government no vain ideas?

from the beginning. (Isaiah 46:10) Because of his accurate foreknowledge of what He will do, he is "Jehovah, who is doing these things, known from of old."—Acts 15:17, 18; Amos 9:12.

[37] In the very book with which the Bible begins, at Genesis 3:15, the Almighty Governor of all creation made known his basic thought regarding the world government that would be the vital need of all earth's inhabitants. In the very book with which the Bible ends, at Revelation 11:15-18, the rightful Governor over all mankind gives prophetic description of his take-over of his long-suspended governorship, saying:

[38] "And the seventh angel blew his trumpet. And loud voices occurred in heaven, saying: 'The kingdom of the world did become the kingdom of our Lord and of his Christ [the woman's "seed" as foretold in Genesis 3:15], and he will rule as king forever and ever.' And the twenty-four elders who were seated before God upon their thrones fell upon their faces and worshiped God, saying: 'We thank you, Jehovah God, the Almighty, the One who is and who was, because you have taken your great power and begun ruling as king. But the nations became wrathful, and your own wrath came, and the appointed time for the dead to be judged, and to give their reward to your slaves the prophets and to the holy ones and to those fearing your name, the small and the great, and to bring to ruin those ruining the earth.' "

[39] As we look at world conditions today, do we not feel that it is high time for the Lord God

---

37, 38. What do Genesis 3:15 and Revelation 11:15-18 show about Jehovah's knowledge regarding government?
39. In what way must Jehovah make his kingdom manifest to us?

Almighty to bring to ruin those ruining the earth? We do not want it to be ruined to the state where we people cannot live on it anymore! It is absolutely necessary for "the kingdom of the world" to become the kingdom of the Lord God Almighty, with "his Christ" as his associate in government. He must rule as king forever and ever, and he must make his kingship manifest to all of us on earth by ruining those who ruin his property, the earth. Revelation 11:15 speaks of it as a dead certainty, as if it had already occurred. That declaration is a divine promise that is beyond recall. It will never fail!

[40] It is a God-given promise that betokens good for all those of our generation who yearn for a united world of mankind under a world government managed by one who faithfully keeps his word. True, he promises things almost unbelievable. He now promises things far greater than the things that were promised to Jehovah's people Israel, more than fifteen centuries before our Common Era. Yet, Jehovah is powerful enough to fulfill such grander things.

[41] To release his enslaved people, Israel, it required Jehovah to break the grip of the Egyptian World Power. Then he had to part the waters of the Red Sea for his liberated people to cross on dry land. He then had to let the waters engulf the pursuing Egyptian cavalrymen and chariots and their haughty Pharaoh. Forty years later Jehovah had to dam up the floodwaters of the Jordan River in order for his people to cross over into the Promised Land. Then for six years he

---

40. Why are his promises, grander than those to Israel, certain?
41, 42. For Joshua 21:44, 45 to be recorded, Jehovah did what exploits?

had to fight in their behalf, tumbling down the walls of Jericho and subduing the larger part of the land so as to apportion it out to the twelve tribes of Israel. In spite of all the formidable obstacles, God, who does not lie, carried out his promise to his people. Testifying to that historical fact, Judge Joshua, the successor of the prophet Moses, recorded the following memorable words:

[42] "All their enemies Jehovah gave into their hand. Not a promise failed out of all the good promise that Jehovah had made to the house of Israel; it all came true."—Joshua 21:44, 45; 23:10.

[43] Now the grand day approaches when the then-living members of our generation will be able to testify that not one promise out of all the good promise of God concerning a righteous world government has failed. He will have made it all come true. So with full confidence in Him we can address ourselves to an examination of his marvelous promises that have to do with world government. Happy will we be if we can finally become his witnesses and say regarding his promise: "It is the truth!"—Isaiah 43:9, 10.

---

43. What time nears when we shall testify, "It is the truth!"?

CHAPTER 3

Predicted World Changes
up till God's Kingdom

"CHANGING TIMES"—those words describe what this generation has been passing through since that epoch-making year of 1914 C.E. As in the view piece of an old-fashioned kaleidoscope when it is turned, the patterns of things have changed. The changes have been to the liking—of how many of us? Not all of us are pleased. We find little pleasure in going contrary to our better inclinations so as to adjust to the unwanted changes. The time for the greatest change of all human experience is at hand! The time is a scheduled one, and fortunately the tremendous change taking place will be under control, for the lasting best interests of all lovers of stable good times.

[2] How can we be sure of this? Today we see mighty political forces that are gathering strength from year to year, bent on changing, as it were, the face of the world. They are convinced that the future of mankind rests within their hands. What we, the average people, would like to have does not concern these world-changing radical forces. A sizable number of people prefer the old way of doing things, of running things, with a large measure of personal choice allowed. Political

1. To what greatest change of all are our times leading?
2. To what forces, intent on change, is resistance still offered?

forces that hold on to the long-practiced way of governing human affairs are still strong, and offer resistance, even though weakening resistance, to the growing forces that aim at uprooting and overturning the old styles of handling mankind's interests.

3 Thus we have the two larger groups on the earthly scene today. The one group in favor of quick, roughshod revolutionary change is quite generally spoken of as the radical party. The other group, which keeps a strong tie with the past and its structures and forms, is quite fittingly called the conservative party. Oddly, we may find that government of a nation that was set up by a violent revolution becomes conservative after quite a length of time. It joins the ranks of the conservatives. It appears that a final showdown fight between the radicals and the conservatives is fast approaching. At present the two political groups are trying to get along with each other. Outwardly, they try to appear cordial to each other. But there are always reservations that are kept in their hearts when they make formal exchanges with each other. Fundamentally, at the bottom of things, they are different. They simply do not mix—no more so than tough iron mixes with a potter's clay.—Daniel 2:43.

4 This is a situation new to human history. It has especially taken form in our twentieth century. Before the world war of 1914-1918, the situation that obtains world wide today was certainly not expected, not predicted. Not even the politicians who consult clairvoyants and astrologers

3. How do the two big political groups treat each other?
4. Before World War I what world situation was not expected?

received any inkling of this back there before the first world war jarred their complacency. Human society so deeply divided politically as it is today, and has been since World War I, was not forevisioned indeed by shortsighted man. But are we aware that this political state of human affairs was prophetically illustrated more than 2,580 years ago, or about the year 605 before our Common Era?

⁵ That ancient date would take us back to the time when Babylon was the world power. In an expression of its world imperialism this Babylonian World Power had destroyed the world-renowned city of Jerusalem and its temple dedicated to the worship of the God of the Hebrews, Jehovah. So far in the distant past it would have been impossible for a clairvoyant, an astrologer or any other mere man to forecast the political state of affairs of our day.

⁶ That has to be admitted by us all!

⁷ Well, then, what proof do we have that anybody in heaven or on earth forecast it? Almost unbelievable as it may seem, we do have such proof. It comes from the One who plotted the course of human government from Babylon's day down till our day. The proof is there to show that the course of such world powers was plotted and that the course plotted for them down till now was followed in human history. All of this had to take into account changes in times and seasons for things of major importance, also the removal of one dynasty of world rulers in favor of a new set of world rulers, even of a different race. It

5, 6. Back in 605 B.C.E. who could not foretell today's situation?
7. Plotting the course of world government belongs to whom?

took into account also the biggest change and transfer of world power that takes place in all human history, the change that is just ahead for this generation of mankind. Such an accurate plotting of the course of world government for mankind calls for someone superhuman, who knows from the beginning the grand finale. It calls for *God,* not the so-called "god of this system of things," but the Almighty God, the All-wise God, man's Creator.—2 Corinthians 4:4; Romans 11:33.

⁸ His plotting of the course or the outline of human history had to be revealed to someone on earth, for him to write it down and put it on record for all of us to consult. That someone was a young Hebrew named Daniel. If he had not been a *worshiper* of the Almighty, All-wise God, this revelation would never have been made to him. He got the import of the revelation made to him. That is why Daniel, in his book of prophecy, wrote down these words of grateful appreciation to the Divine Source of his information:

⁹ "Let the name of God become blessed from time indefinite even to time indefinite, for wisdom and mightiness—for they belong to him. And he is changing times and seasons, removing kings and setting up kings, giving wisdom to the wise ones and knowledge to those knowing discernment. He is revealing the deep things and the concealed things, knowing what is in the darkness; and with him the light does dwell. To you, O God of my forefathers, I am giving praise and commendation,

8, 9. (a) To whom was this outline of human history revealed? (b) What did he say in appreciation to his Source of information?

because wisdom and mightiness you have given to me. And now you have made known to me what we requested of you, for you have made known to us the very matter of the king."—Daniel 2:20-23.

[10] When the prophet Daniel revealed to the forgetful ruler of Babylon the forgotten "matter of the king," this highest politician of the time, Nebuchadnezzar, was honest enough to admit that only the Most High God could make such a revelation concerning the then dark and concealed future. In deep respect he said to Daniel:

[11] "Truly the God of you men is a God of gods and a Lord of kings and a Revealer of secrets, because you were able to reveal this secret."—Daniel 2:47.

[12] What political ruler today, after reading Daniel's account of the revealed secret and then comparing this with the course of world government till now, would make such an acknowledgment concerning the God of Daniel and of his three Hebrew companions? In vain we look for such an honest, self-humbling political ruler who shows that he is letting the secret revealed to Daniel guide his own course of action. Therefore the worldwide change that is to be brought about shortly by the Divine Changer of times and seasons will come upon them all with crushing force.

[13] What was it that convinced the prophet Daniel as well as the leading politician of the day, King Nebuchadnezzar of Babylon, that the

---

10, 11. When told his dream, what did Nebuchadnezzar say of God?
12. How do politicians of today differ from Nebuchadnezzar?
13. To whom did Nebuchadnezzar appeal about his forgotten dream?

One who could give such a preview of thousands of years of human history and thus be "declaring the end from the beginning" had to be God Almighty? (Isaiah 46:10, *Authorized Version*) It was the humanly impossible requirements that stood in the way of such a revelation. In the second year of his reign as the conqueror of Jerusalem with its temple of Jehovah's worship, he had a dream. On awakening from sleep, he could not remember it. He was deeply agitated over the matter, because the forgotten dream seemed to convey a message of supreme importance to him. He put his astrologers and magic-practicing priests to an abnormal test by demanding that they should, not only interpret the dream, but, first of all, recall it to the king's mind. Because they called such a demand wholly unreasonable, King Nebuchadnezzar ordered them to be put to death as being frauds in their prophetical profession. But that he was mentally unbalanced in making such a decision even the most prominent psychologist of today may agree.

[14] The dire emergency now existing affected the prophet Daniel, because he was considered foremost among the wise men of Babylon. He asked the king's bodyguard officer why he had come to kill him and his three Hebrew companions, Hananiah, Mishael and Azariah. On being informed, Daniel asked for just a day's extension of the time of execution of Babylon's wise men. He had confidence that nothing was impossible for his God, Jehovah. The combined prayers of Daniel and his three Hebrew companions did not

14. How did Daniel get the needed lifesaving information?

prove to be directed to a false, mythical god. Both Nebuchadnezzar's dream and its world-important meaning were revealed to Daniel in a prophetic "night vision" sent by his God Jehovah. (Daniel 2:19) After blessing the Doer of humanly impossible things and giving credit to Him, Daniel asked Arioch the chief of King Nebuchadnezzar's bodyguard to present him to the perplexed emperor of the Babylonian Empire.

¹⁵ The lives of Daniel and of his three Hebrew companions were at stake. If he did not recall to the emperor's mind the forgotten dream and then, on this basis, give a satisfying explanation, they would have to be executed with all of Babylon's wise men. This forced a test, not of a man, but of the real God of the universe, for Babylon's astrologers and magic-practicing priests had already failed. In what Daniel now disclosed to the ruler of the Babylonian World Power, he became outstandingly a witness of Jehovah, one of Jehovah's pre-Christian witnesses. (Isaiah 43:10-12; 44:8) As an excellent example for all modern-day witnesses of Jehovah, Daniel took no credit to himself for what he was now about to disclose to the world's most prominent politician, but gave the glory to the real "God in the heavens" by saying:

¹⁶ "The secret that the king himself is asking, the wise men, the conjurers, the magic-practicing priests and the astrologers themselves are unable to show to the king. However, there exists a God in the heavens who is a Revealer of secrets,

---

15, 16. This forced a test of whom, and to whom did Daniel give credit?

and he has made known to King Nebuchadnezzar what is to occur in the final part of the days. Your dream and the visions of your head upon your bed—this it is."—Daniel 2:27, 28.

[17] If Nebuchadnezzar's dream had been a mere idle, meaningless dream such as occurs to anybody, it would never have been recorded in Jehovah's Word, the Bible. It was a purposeful dream sent by the Divine "Revealer of secrets," but it would be meaningless if it could not be explained. And yet, the God Almighty of the heavens blotted out all memory of the dream in Nebuchadnezzar's mind. Was not Jehovah defeating his purpose in doing this, in making the king's memory a blank? Not at all. Rather, he was laying the basis for magnifying his own superhuman power. He was posing a problem that only a god, only the true God, could solve.

[18] By his way of handling the matter of such world importance, Jehovah made it necessary for the testimony of divine power to be given to the earthly "king of kings" of that ancient day. The king was driven to use his absolute authority and ask for the recall of the dream and its interpretation. He asked for it, and he had to take it when it was miraculously given to him. Whether Nebuchadnezzar liked it or not, he got what he demanded. Thus, at the start of unopposed rulership by the Babylonian World Power, this topmost politician had proved to him that there is a God, that God is!—Daniel 2:1, 28.

---

17. How did Jehovah magnify his power as "Revealer of secrets"?
18. How was the king forced into proving that God is?

THE DREAM OF WORLD-POWER CHANGES

[19] There is an old saying: "Man proposes, but God disposes." This is true with regard to world affairs. The Creator of heaven and earth is really concerned about world affairs upon our earth. He has an interest in what goes on here, because the earth on which we live is His, not the rightful domain of world communism or of capital-owning democracy. That His interests in the earth come foremost and will finally be claimed and cared for, Jehovah illustrated in the dream his prophet Daniel re-revealed to King Nebuchadnezzar of Babylon in the heyday of its power, when it was inclined to claim all the earth as subject to conquest by it. With the greatest of attention, the king listened to God's Word and took it seriously, as Jehovah's prophet Daniel went on to say:

[20] "You, O king, happened to be beholding, and, look! a certain immense image. That image, which was large and the brightness of which was extraordinary, was standing in front of you, and its appearance was dreadful. As regards that image, its head was of good gold, its breasts and its arms were of silver, its belly and its thighs were of copper, its legs were of iron, its feet were partly of iron and partly of molded clay. You kept on looking until a stone was cut out not by hands, and it struck the image on its feet of iron and of molded clay and crushed them. At that time the iron, the molded clay, the copper, the silver and the gold were, all together, crushed and became like the chaff from the summer threshing floor, and the wind carried them away so that no trace

19. What will Jehovah show politicians about claims to the earth?
20. What was the dream that Daniel recalled to the king?

at all was found of them. And as for the stone that struck the image, it became a large mountain and filled the whole earth."—Daniel 2:31-35.

21 We can imagine how startled King Nebuchadnezzar was at this inspired description. It fitted exactly the dream as he had seen it! This large image that was of such dazzling brightness was one that inspired fear, dread, and was terrible for its impressiveness. How could he ever have forgotten it? But he did! If the dream of it were never recalled, the message that it was designed to convey would be forever lost. Being sent, evidently by divine power, to him who was then the world's "king of kings," it must have some timely message of worldwide consequence. Only God could have reproduced in a vision by night to Daniel what had completely vanished from Nebuchadnezzar's mind. But could the same God explain the meaning of the forgotten dream? Surely the God who framed and sent the dream ought to know what he meant by it. He could tell what the humanlike image meant, from head to toe. By giving a complete dream, which revealed how the meaningful image was disposed of, he demonstrated that He knew and was "declaring the end from the beginning." So 'carry on,' O Daniel!

22 Merely disclosing the prophetic dream was not enough. The explaining of it as well was what would cause Daniel and all the other wise men of Babylon to be spared from death. Daniel had an explanation of the dream image, but would his

21. How did God thus show he knew "the end" from the "beginning"?
22. Why are we more interested in the dream than the king was?

interpretation satisfy King Nebuchadnezzar, a pagan ruler who had destroyed Jehovah's temple at Jerusalem, as being right? Is it an interpretation that satisfies us today, as being not only reasonable and logical but also in harmony with all the rest of God's revealed Word, the inspired Bible? We today, who are evidently living at the time of "the end" of the dream's fulfillment ought to be more interested than Nebuchadnezzar, who was living at the time of the "beginning" of the dream's coming true. He was not threatened with the worldwide smashup yet to take place. We are!

[23] Arioch, the chief of Nebuchadnezzar's body-guard, may have relaxed his grip on his sword as Daniel went on to say to his military Commander in Chief: "This is the dream, and its interpretation we shall say before the king. You, O king, the king of kings, you to whom the God of heaven has given the kingdom, the might, and the strength and the dignity, and into whose hand he has given, wherever the sons of mankind are dwelling, the beasts of the field and the winged creatures of the heavens, and whom he has made ruler over all of them, you yourself are the head of gold."—Daniel 2:36-38.

[24] Nebuchadnezzar's being told at the beginning of the explanation of the image that it involved him and really started with him should have heightened his interest in the interpretation of the whole dream. His being told that he was symbolized by a head made of the most precious metal then known could hardly do otherwise than

---

23. Whom did Daniel say the golden head of the image pictured? Why?
24. So, then, did the "image" begin with Babylon's founder?

please him and make him feel that due dignity was being accorded to him. The golden head fittingly represented an emperor, the "king of kings" whom the God of heaven had permitted to become the commanding world figure, the ruler of the Babylonian World Power. Thus the thing that was pictured by the image of four different metals did not begin with Nimrod the Cushite of the Hamitic race, who founded the original Babel or Babylon more than 1,500 years earlier.—Genesis 10:8-10; 1 Chronicles 1:10.

[25] Also, the symbolic image did not begin with the Egyptian World Power, a Hamitic empire that was the First World Power taken note of in the Bible record. (Genesis 10:6, 13, 14; 12:11 through 13:1; Psalms 78:51; 105:23, 27; 106:21, 22) Further, the symbolic image did not begin with the Assyrian World Power, a Shemitic empire that became the Second World Power of Bible record. (Genesis 10:21, 22; 2:14; 25:18; 2 Kings 15:19-29) In 632 B.C.E. Nebuchadnezzar shared in overthrowing the Assyrian World Power and thereby set up the Neo-Babylonian Empire, which ranked as the Third World Power of Bible record.—Nahum 2:8 through 3:18; Zephaniah 2:13.

[26] About twenty-five years later, after Emperor Nebuchadnezzar was used as Jehovah's instrument to destroy unfaithful Jerusalem, the prophet Daniel's words applied: "Into [your] hand he [the God of heaven] has given, wherever the sons of mankind are dwelling, the beasts of the field and the winged creatures of the heavens,

---

25. Did it start with the First World Power, or the second?
26. Why did the "image" apply from Jerusalem's destruction on?

and [you] he has made ruler over all of them."
(Daniel 2:38) This was the case, because, with
the destruction of Jerusalem by the Babylonians
in 607 B.C.E., a typical kingdom of Jehovah God
ceased to exist on earth.—1 Chronicles 29:23;
2 Chronicles 36:17-21.

[27] Inasmuch as Daniel said to Nebuchadnezzar,
"You yourself are the head of gold," the metallic
image as a whole pictured a series of emperors
or world rulers. Really, the "head of gold" pictured more than Nebuchadnezzar himself. It pictured the ruling dynasty that was established in
him. Thus the golden head pictured, in full,
Nebuchadnezzar himself, then his oldest son Evil-
merodach, then Nabonidus the son-in-law of
Nebuchadnezzar, and finally Belshazzar the grandson of Nebuchadnezzar. (2 Kings 25:27-30; Jeremiah 52:31-34; Daniel 5:10, 11, 18, 22) This
dynasty stood as representative of the Babylonian
World Power. Accordingly, the series of four
metals in the image of Nebuchadnezzar's dream
represents a series of world powers that have
exercised world domination without interference
from God's kingdom (either the typical earthly
kingdom or the antitypical heavenly kingdom).
Daniel's interpretation of the dream proves this
point.

[28] Pointing to the world domination that was
to be exercised by the successors to the Babylonian
World Power, Daniel went on with his interpretation, saying to Nebuchadnezzar, the "king
of kings": "And after you there will rise another
kingdom inferior to you; and another kingdom, a

---

27. Each metal of the "image" pictures what, politically?
28, 29. Why was the next kingdom, inferior to Babylon, not
named?

third one, of copper, that will rule over the whole earth."—Daniel 2:39.

²⁹ Daniel did not name that kingdom, "inferior" to Nebuchadnezzar, that was to follow right after the Babylonian World Power. Naming it would have put the Babylonian World Power on guard against the future aspirant to world domination. But from the earlier prophecies of Isaiah (13:1-17; 21:2-9) Daniel could have known that the Medes, the allies of the Persians, would be involved in the toppling of Babylon from her high position of world power.

³⁰ Daniel could also know from Isaiah 44:24 through 45:7 that Jehovah would use a man named Cyrus, who proved to be a Persian, to bring divine vengeance upon the Babylonian World Power for destroying Jerusalem and its temple of Jehovah's worship. (Isaiah 46:11) As a student of Jeremiah's prophecy also, Daniel knew that the Medes would be prominent in the final siege of Babylon and would have a part in overthrowing this persecutor of his people. (Jeremiah 51:28; Daniel 9:2) But Daniel did not then disclose this information to Nebuchadnezzar, who would not live to see that overthrow. Why should he be made to worry?

³¹ The prophet Daniel had the privilege to introduce, as it were, the "kingdom" or world power that was symbolized by the silver of the dream image. This was on that autumn night in 539 B.C.E. when Nebuchadnezzar's grandson, King Belshazzar, was holding a royal banquet with a thousand of his grandees inside the besieged city

30. How could Daniel know about the overthrower of Babylon?
31. How was Daniel privileged to introduce Babylon's successor?

of Babylon. At the height of their feasting a miraculous hand wrote upon the wall the enigmatic words "Mene, Mene, Tekel and Parsin." As a last recourse, terrified King Belshazzar had to summon Daniel to interpret this handwriting on the wall. In explaining the last word "Parsin," which is the plural of the word "Peres," Daniel said to Belshazzar: "PERES, your kingdom has been divided and given to the Medes and the Persians." That same night the besiegers gained entrance into Babylon, King Belshazzar was killed, and the Medo-Persian World Power was set up. As the Medes and the Persians were Aryans, world power now shifted from the Shemitic race to the Japhetic race.—Daniel 5:1-31; 6:12; Esther 1:19.

[32] As silver is inferior to gold, the Medo-Persian World Power was inferior to the Babylonian. In what way? In that it did not exalt itself so high as did the Babylonian Empire, which destroyed the city of Jerusalem and its temple for Jehovah's worship. Thus the king of Babylon, Nebuchadnezzar, appeared to exalt himself above Jehovah God, whose name was called upon the city of Jerusalem where the kings of David's royal line sat upon "Jehovah's throne." (1 Chronicles 29:23; Isaiah 14:4-14) Also, with that overthrow of Jehovah's typical kingdom in the year 607 B.C.E., the period of 2,520 years known as "the times of the Gentiles" or "appointed times of the nations" took its start. (Luke 21:24, *AV; NW*) Instead of trying to "resemble the Most High," King Cyrus the conqueror of Babylon recognized Jehovah's Godship.

---

32. In what way was Medo-Persia "inferior" to Babylon?

³³ In recognition of the expressed will of Jehovah, King Cyrus tried to harmonize his course of action with what Jehovah had prophesied concerning him in Isaiah, chapters forty-four and forty-five. So, in 537 B.C.E., he let a band of Israelite volunteers and their attendants leave their Babylonish prison and return to their homeland, to rebuild the city of Jerusalem and its holy temple. But the typical kingdom of Jehovah was not reestablished there, with a royal descendant of King David sitting on "Jehovah's throne" at Jerusalem.—2 Chronicles 36:20-23; Ezra 1:1 through 2:2.

GRECIAN (MACEDONIAN) WORLD POWER

³⁴ Notwithstanding its considerations in a merciful way to Jehovah's chosen people, the Persian World Power was not to last down till our twentieth century. Concerning the immediate successor to the Medo-Persian World Power, the prophet Daniel went on to say to Nebuchadnezzar: "And another kingdom, a third one, of copper, that will rule over the whole earth."—Daniel 2:39.

³⁵ Those words would indicate that the "third," copper-like, "kingdom" or world power would be more extensive than either the Medo-Persian or the Babylonian World Power. As copper is a semiprecious metal, inferior to silver, this upcoming world power would be inferior to the Medo-Persian World Power. In this respect it was not honored with any privilege like that of liberating Jehovah's exiled people from their im-

---

33. How did Cyrus harmonize his course with Isaiah's prophecy?
34. What did interpreter Daniel say of Medo-Persia's successor?
35. When did Daniel learn the identity of Medo-Persia's successor?

prisonment in Babylon. In the days of Nebuchadnezzar's grandson, King Belshazzar, Daniel the interpreter of dreams learned just who would establish that copper-like "third" world power. It would be a Grecian conqueror. There is no evidence that Daniel disclosed this information concerning far future days to King Belshazzar.

[36] In explaining the prophetic dream that was sent to Daniel in which he saw a two-horned ram being overpowered by a one-horned hairy goat, Jehovah's holy angel said: "The ram that you saw possessing the two horns stands for the kings of Media and Persia. And the hairy he-goat stands for the king of Greece [or, Hellas]; and as for the great horn that was between its eyes, it stands for the first king. And that one having been broken, so that there were four that finally stood up instead of it, there are four kingdoms from his nation that will stand up, but not with his power."—Daniel 8:20-22.

[37] Thus, more than two hundred years in advance, it was foretold that the "kingdom" that was symbolized by the copper belly and thighs of the dream image would be the Grecian World Power. Its "first king" proved to be the world conqueror, Alexander III of Macedonia, who set out to conquer the Persian Empire. In 334 B.C.E. he handed a decisive crushing defeat to the then Persian emperor and established the Grecian (Macedonian) World Power. In 332 B.C.E. Alexander the Great brought the province of Judea, including Jerusalem, under his control. Thereafter Egypt fell to him, and the city of Alexandria was

36. How was Medo-Persia's overthrow pictured to Daniel?
37. What exploits did the Grecian Empire's "first king" perform?

founded there in order to memorialize his name. This new Egyptian seaport became very prosperous, and it came to have a sizable Jewish population.

[38] Because of his conquests all the way over to the Indus River of India and down into Egypt, and his establishing military garrisons in the conquered lands, the common Greek spoken by the troops of Alexander the Great became the international language of the day. It served as the media for international communication, and in the third century B.C.E. the Greek-speaking Jews of Alexandria, Egypt, began translating the inspired Hebrew Scriptures into the common Greek. This lead was followed by the inspired writers who produced the twenty-seven books of the Christian Scriptures, from Matthew to Revelation. In this way it became possible for the inspired Bible as a whole to be read universally by speakers and readers of the common Greek.

[39] In the year 323 B.C.E., Alexander the Great, symbolized by the "great horn" of the hairy he-goat, died at Babylon, the onetime capital of the Babylonian Empire. In course of time his vast empire was divided up between four of his Grecian generals. This resulted in four Hellenic or Grecianized kingdoms. Judea and Jerusalem eventually became part of the kingdom begun by General Seleucus I Nicator. Of course, none of these four Hellenic kingdoms compared with the great empire of Alexander the Great. Marvelously, indeed, the prophecy was fulfilled that out of the "great horn" (Alexander the Great) there would come 'four horns' (four Hellenic kingdoms), but none

---

38. How did it become possible to read the whole Bible in Greek?
39. How did "four kingdoms" of Greek style arise as prophesied?

of these four possessing the power and magnitude of Alexander's empire. Nevertheless, these four minor kingdoms together maintained the domination of the Grecian World Power, symbolized by the copper part of the image.

THE IRONLIKE KINGDOM

⁴⁰ Time passed on into the first century before our Common Era. The time came for "the God of heaven," Jehovah, to change times and seasons and to remove kings and to set up kings for the bringing in of a new world power. (Daniel 2:19, 21) Rome, Italy, was now the upcoming political power with which to reckon. In the year 63 B.C.E. Roman General Pompey captured Jerusalem and extended Roman control over Judea. In the year 30 B.C.E. a decisive defeat was administered to the last of the four Hellenic kingdoms, and Egypt became a Roman province. This marked the setting up of the Roman World Power in the five hundred and seventy-seventh year of the "times of the Gentiles" or "appointed times of the nations." Jerusalem continued to be without a king of the royal line of David of the tribe of Judah. "Jehovah's throne" was no longer standing at the Jewish capital Jerusalem.—1 Chronicles 29:23.

⁴¹ Here we see the fulfillment of what the prophet Daniel had told King Nebuchadnezzar when interpreting the forgotten dream of the image that was made up of four metals. In interpreting the meaning of the fourth metal, iron, of which the legs of the image were made, Daniel said: "And as for the fourth kingdom, it will prove to

40. How was the Roman World Power set up by 30 B.C.E.?
41. What did Daniel explain the fourth metal, iron, to be?

be strong like iron. Forasmuch as iron is crushing and grinding everything else, so, like iron that shatters, it will crush and shatter even all these."—Daniel 2:40.

[42] The Roman World Power crushed the Grecian World Power and swallowed up remnants of the preceding Medo-Persian and Babylonian World Powers. It showed no respect for the "kingdom of the heavens," "the kingdom of God," that was proclaimed by Jesus Christ and his first-century disciples. In the year 33 C.E. it desecrated the Jewish Passover Day by putting Jesus Christ to death on a torture stake outside the walls of Jerusalem. Further, in the year 64 C.E., after the burning of part of the city of Rome, it began persecuting the faithful disciples of Jesus Christ, in this way trying to crush and shatter true Christianity.

[43] In the year 70 C.E., in its effort to put down the revolt of the rebellious Jews, Rome found it necessary to crush and shatter Jerusalem, reducing it and its magnificent temple to ruins. The 97,000 unchristianized Jews that managed to survive that horrible destruction of their holy city were distributed as captive slaves to the widespread parts of the Roman Empire. This occurred in the six hundred and seventy-sixth year of the "times of the Gentiles," and left 1,844 years yet to go to the end of the Gentile Times.

[44] Jesus Christ, in the course of foretelling the destruction of Jerusalem by the Romans under

42. How did the Roman Empire show no respect for Kingdom preachers?
43. When and why did the Roman Empire destroy Jerusalem?
44, 45. What did the Gentiles' trampling on Jerusalem really mean?

General Titus, the son of Emperor Vespasian, said: "And they [the Jews in the Roman province of Judea] will fall by the edge of the sword and be led captive into all the nations; and Jerusalem will be trampled on by the nations, until the appointed times of the nations are fulfilled." (Luke 21:20-24) By those words Jesus Christ did not mean the trampling down of the mere site of the city by the non-Jewish or Gentile nations. Back there the city of Jerusalem stood for more than what Jerusalem of today, the capital of the Republic of Israel, with its democratically elected president and its Knesset, represents. Back there in Christ's day, Jerusalem with its temple represented "the city of the great King," Jehovah. (Matthew 5:35; 4:5) This onetime throne-city of Jehovah's typical kingdom on earth was a symbol of God's kingdom under the rule of his anointed king of the royal family of David.

[45] And so the Messianic kingdom, to which the royal descendants of David held the title, is the thing that was to be trampled on by the Gentiles until the "appointed times of the nations" for this trampling to occur without God's interference ended. The end of the Gentile Times is where our twentieth century comes into account!

ANOTHER WORLD POWER INCLUDED

[46] As we look back from our twentieth century, we ask: Is that "fourth kingdom" as pictured by the iron legs of Nebuchadnezzar's dream image fulfilled to completion in just the Roman Empire or World Power? The Bible itself indicates that this was not to be the case. How so? In the days

46. Did Roman Emperor Constantine bring in God's kingdom?

of Emperor Constantine in the fourth century, the Roman Empire became "Christian," but this was merely by imperial decree and in name only. This change of religious complexion did not create a new world power, a Christian world power; it did not bring the kingdom of God as preached by Jesus Christ. However, a new world power did come after the passage of many centuries—in a really *political* way. This was indicated in the last book of the Bible, in Revelation 17:9, 10.

[47] There, with reference to the religious harlot, Babylon the Great, as riding a wild beast with seven heads and ten horns, we read: "Here is where the intelligence that has wisdom comes in: The seven heads mean seven mountains, where the woman sits on top. And there are seven kings: five have fallen, one is, the other has not yet arrived, but when he does arrive he must remain a short while." From this explanation of the symbols here found in the book of Revelation, the wild beast pictures a political system on earth. The seven heads of the wild beast represent headship over the political system, not headship of all seven at one time, but headship by one symbolic head after the other until the seventh and last head. Fittingly the seven heads represent "seven mountains," that dominate the earth below. Quite nicely, also, the seven heads represent "seven kings," for kings are the heads of State and exercise headship or domination. Like in Nebuchadnezzar's dream image, the kings stand for kingdoms or world powers.

[48] As to the "seven kings," the Christian apostle John wrote near the close of the first century C.E.:

---

47. What do the seven heads of the "wild beast" picture?
48. Who were the five "kings" that fell previous to Rome?

"Five have fallen, one is." (Revelation 17:10) At the time that John wrote the Revelation he was held as a prisoner on the penal island of Patmos for being a Christian. (Revelation 1:1, 2, 9) So, when writing, "Five have fallen, one is," John points to a sixth "king." That one *was* in John's day. So, then, which world power is it that John designates by the expression "one is"? No one else but the Roman World Power. Here it is ranked as the Sixth World Power according to Bible prophecy. Who, then, were the five "kings" that had fallen prior to the Roman World Power, one by one? First, the Egyptian World Power; second, the Assyrian World Power; third, the Babylonian World Power; fourth, the Medo-Persian World Power; and, fifth, the Grecian World Power.

[49] However, the Sixth World Power was also to fall, for the angel said to the apostle John: "One is, the other has not yet arrived." (Revelation 17:10) This signified that a seventh world power was yet to come, to correspond with the seventh head of the wild beast. In the apostle John's day that 'seventh head,' or 'seventh mountain,' or 'seventh king' was a mystery. But centuries of world history since John's day have unraveled the mystery. What, then, is the Seventh World Power of Bible prophecy? It came forth in the year 1763 C.E., in the form of the British Empire, the Britannia that ruled the seven seas.

[50] Twelve years later, in 1775, the thirteen American colonies broke away from the British Empire, to set up the American Republic, the United States of America. In the process of time

49. At whose hands did the sixth "king" fall, and when?
50. How did the Anglo-American Dual World Power come to be?

the English-speaking American Republic found it advisable to work together with the English-speaking British Empire, both in peacetime and in wartime, a thing that was emphasized during World Wars I and II. In actuality, then, there has been a British-American Dual World Power. So, for many years now since the American Revolution of 1775-1783 this Anglo-American political combination has been the Seventh World Power. It acts like a two-horned beast.—Revelation 13:11.

[51] The Seventh World Power "arrived" in Jehovah's time for a change before the establishment of his own Messianic kingdom. Concerning the Seventh World Power, Revelation 17:10 says: "But when he does arrive he must remain a short while." The American section of the Seventh World Power has just celebrated its two hundredth anniversary. This is relatively "a short while" in comparison with the duration of the Roman World Power for nearly eighteen hundred years. By now that "short while" should be about ended, according to Jehovah's timetable. One thing is certain from the Bible prophecy: The Messianic kingdom of God was not booked to come until first that Seventh World Power had come on the worldly scene. (Revelation 17:11-14) In view of all of this, it becomes very plain that the iron legs of Nebuchadnezzar's dream image picture more than the Roman World Power. They picture also the political outgrowth from that Roman Empire, namely, the Anglo-American World Power, the Seventh World Power, which has proved

---

51. Why did the legs of iron picture more than the Roman Empire?

to be the greatest world power of them all from a human standpoint. It too has been like iron, steel!

FEET PARTLY OF IRON AND PARTLY OF CLAY

[52] Now to the final features of the prophetic dream that the king of Babylon dreamed but forgot. King Nebuchadnezzar wanted to know what the climax of the dream meant, and so do we today. Thanks to Jehovah God, Daniel was inspired to explain matters further, saying: "And whereas you beheld the feet and the toes to be partly of molded clay of a potter and partly of iron, the kingdom itself will prove to be divided, but somewhat of the hardness of iron will prove to be in it, forasmuch as you beheld the iron mixed with moist clay. And as for the toes of the feet being partly of iron and partly of molded clay, the kingdom will partly prove to be strong and will partly prove to be fragile. Whereas you beheld iron mixed with moist clay, they will come to be mixed with the offspring of mankind; but they will not prove to be sticking together, this one to that one, just as iron is not mixing with molded clay."—Daniel 2:41-43.

[53] In those prophetic words is given us the illustration of a divided kingdom. Since this is the way in which the symbolic image of successive world powers ends up, this state of divided world power is what should be the case today, in our own twentieth century. It is! For this valid reason we should be near to the passing away of this long-standing symbolic image of world power. When

---

52. What did Daniel say of the feet partly of iron and partly of clay?
53. What state of political affairs do such feet picture? When?

finally the symbolic image does pass away, what next? According to the "wise men" of this world, such a passing would be the worst thing that could happen. In their view, it would mean anarchy, chaos. So they try to keep the image standing.

⁵⁴ The world scene is still under the shadow of the Seventh World Power, both sections of which are mightily armed with nuclear bombs and missiles to deliver them. So there still remains in the dominant system of rulership the strength of iron with its ability to crush and shatter. But this Anglo-American World Power, together with its allies, has another factor, a more modern factor, with which to contend. This factor was pictured by the moist molded clay in Nebuchadnezzar's dream image. What does it picture in the light of our modern day? Daniel's explanation says for our illumination: "They will come to be mixed with the offspring of mankind; but they will not prove to be sticking together, this one to that one, just as iron is not mixing with molded clay." Accordingly, the molded clay symbolizes "the offspring of mankind," or, literally, 'the seed of men.'—Daniel 2:43.

⁵⁵ Clay is quite a suitable symbol of the 'seed of men,' for Job 4:19 speaks of humans as "those dwelling in houses of clay, whose foundation is in the dust." And the greatly afflicted man Job said to Jehovah God: "Remember, please, that out of clay you have made me and to dust you will make me return." (Job 10:9) Despite the fragile nature of "clay" of which the "offspring of mankind" are made, the trend of human rulership in these last

54. What does Daniel indicate that the molded clay pictures?
55. How has there been a mixing with the "offspring of mankind"?

decades of its existence has been in which direction? No, not to God the Creator of the animated "clay," but to the creatures of clay, to the common people, the "proletariat" as the ancient Romans called the lowest or poorest class of people who contributed nothing but offspring (*prolēs*) to the political State. The old traditional rulership has been obliged to listen more and more to the clamor of the common people for a share in governments over them.

[56] However, there can be no marriage between the old aristocratic, authoritarian style of government and the common people who favor radical, thoroughgoing changes in government. No more so than there can be an amalgamation of iron with clay! The making of governments democratic by revolutions or otherwise has led on to radical proletarian forms of government. And these latter stand in an uncompromising opposition to the ironlike Seventh World Power, the Anglo-American Dual World Power. Till now the two forms of rulership have managed to live alongside each other, but there has been no real marriage between them. The radical, proletarian governments and blocs may appear to be very strong and seemingly outmaneuvering the Anglo-American World Power in strength. Yet they are just as fragile as human creatures of clay, who support radical governments. They cannot strengthen the symbolic image of world rulership to resist the next world change.

---

56. Why is there no marriage between the iron and the clay?

CHAPTER 4

How God's Kingdom Becomes a World Government

THE symbolic "image" of world rulership by human politics—its gold, its silver, its copper, its iron and its clay—is doomed as a whole! Jehovah God, who foretold the end from the beginning, says so in his prophetic Word. Let us take note from that Word that it is not the divided condition of the feet and toes that causes the downfall of the "image." It is not any nuclear global war between the symbolic "iron" and the symbolic "clay" that brings about the destruction of the "image" from head to foot. The prophetic dream as recalled to Nebuchadnezzar's mind by Jehovah's prophet Daniel plainly shows that the destruction does not come from within the "image," but comes from outside it. From where, then? Daniel indicated this when he ended his interpretation, saying to King Nebuchadnezzar:

² "And in the days of those kings the God of heaven will set up a kingdom that will never be brought to ruin. And the kingdom itself will not be passed on to any other people. It will crush

―――――――――
1, 2. Destruction of the "image" comes how—from within or from without?

and put an end to all these kingdoms, and it itself will stand to times indefinite; forasmuch as you beheld that out of the mountain a stone was cut not by hands, and that it crushed the iron, the copper, the molded clay, the silver and the gold. The grand God himself has made known to the king what is to occur after this. And the dream is reliable, and the interpretation of it is trustworthy."—Daniel 2:44, 45.

[3] We today, who can look back over more than 2,580 years of time from Nebuchadnezzar's dream, have far more reason to believe, than Nebuchadnezzar ever had, that the dream is reliable in meaning and that its interpretation by Daniel is trustworthy. Hence we are led to believing the word of "the grand God." And so, from where does destruction of the symbolic "image" come? From "the God of heaven," the One who changes the times and seasons and who puts down kings and sets up other kings according to his own will. The fixed time for him to do so must be very near. Why so? Because back in early autumn of the year 1914 C.E., the last year of the Gentile Times, "the appointed times of the nations" ended. According to Christ's words in Luke 21:20-24, this meant that the time had arrived for God to stop the further trampling by the nations on what Jerusalem symbolized. How?

[4] In the summer of 1914 world war broke out between the Seventh World Power and the principal leftover parts of the previous Sixth World Power, for some time known as the Holy Roman Empire of the German Nation. The main issue

3. Why must the time for God to make changes be near?
4. How did God react to clergy prayers regarding World War I?

in dispute was world domination here on earth, a quarter of which the British Empire then controlled. God's Messianic kingdom was of no interest or concern to the warring disputants. And yet they were fighting over that to which God's Messianic kingdom (as pictured by Jerusalem of Bible times) held the title, namely, world rulership. The clergy of Christendom prayed in favor of both sides engaged in the global conflict. But did Jehovah God pay attention to the clergy's patriotic, nationalistic prayers? Not for a moment! According to the prophetic picture given in Revelation 12:1-10, at the close of the Gentile Times in 1914 Jehovah God brought to birth up in the heavens his promised Messianic kingdom in the hands of his enthroned Son, Jesus Christ.

⁵ This is how the "stone" in Nebuchadnezzar's dream was cut out of the mountain without the aid of human hands. The Messianic kingdom in the hands of the glorified Jesus Christ is the "stone" of the dream. That long-promised kingdom could come forth only from the "God of heaven," Jehovah, the Sovereign Lord.

⁶ So the "mountain" out of which the stone is miraculously cut is not one of the "seven mountains" upon which the religious harlot, Babylon the Great, has been sitting as an empress. (Revelation 17:9, 10) The symbolic "mountain" is not an earthly mountain of rulership. It is a universal "mountain" of rulership, for it is the universal sovereignty of the Creator of heaven and earth, namely, Jehovah "the grand God." (Psalm 121:1, 2; Daniel 2:45) The royal "stone" was cut out

---

5, 6. Out of what mountain was the "stone" cut? When, and how?

by divine power from the universal "mountain" at the close of the Gentile Times in 1914 C.E. Since then God's Messianic kingdom has a right to interfere in the affairs of the nations and to have "this good news of the kingdom" preached in all the inhabited earth "for a witness to all the nations" before their end comes. (Matthew 24:3-14) The Kingdom is now in action!

7 In that war-shocked year of 1914 there were more rulers sitting on thrones as kings than at present. There the circumstances existed for the words of Daniel 2:44 to be true: "In the days of those kings the God of heaven will set up a kingdom that will never be brought to ruin." Those "kings," or whatever political rulers have since come to power on earth, have refused to pay attention to the "good news of the kingdom" that has now been given a worldwide publication. They, or their governments, have opposed or even violently persecuted the Christian preachers of the "good news" of Jehovah's established Messianic kingdom. This, such "kings" have done as an expression of their being determined to hold on to their earthly sovereignties. What, then, has to be done with regard to such rulers who refuse to cede their sovereignties to the Messianic kingdom that God has put in power? Daniel 2:44 gives us the answer:

8 "And the kingdom itself will not be passed on to any other people. It will crush and put an end to all these kingdoms, and it itself will stand to times indefinite." Such a thing will mean the total end of this system of things. It will mean

7. How have "those kings" shown determination to keep ruling?
8. The thing done to the "image" means what for our system?

the everlasting disappearance of the symbolic "image" of man-made political world powers. This is just ahead, nearer now than ever before since 1914 C.E. The removal of the idolized "image" of human rulership will not be a peaceful one. There will be a crushing and grinding of it to powder. As the Messianic Kingdom "stone" enters, as it were, the atmosphere of our earth on its God-given mission, it will not explode like some meteorite from outer space. With the full force of all the momentum that it has picked up since 1914, this indestructible "stone" of diamondlike hardness will reach its objective with a smashing impact. Where?

[9] On the "feet" of the symbolic "image," the "feet" of iron and moist clay that are still standing today. We, this generation of mankind, are living "in the days of those kings," in the days of these partly iron, partly clay "feet." We, this generation of post-Gentile Times, are about to witness the crashing of the Kingdom "stone" against the Seventh World Power and all the other political governments inside or outside the United Nations organization. Thus, in a final clash over the supreme issue of universal sovereignty, the Kingdom "stone" will put an end forever to "all these kingdoms." What will that mean to us who are of this generation that will be caught right in the middle of this crash? Have we ever thought about that?

[10] The violent putting of an end to this earth-wide system of man-made political rulership will not leave a vacuum here as far as government

---

9. What crash will this post-Gentile Times generation witness?
10. Why does the end of man rule leave no governmental vacuum?

for humankind is concerned. Nebuchadnezzar's prophetic dream does not show that a government-less emptiness will set in on the earth in which every human inhabitant will do just as he pleases without submission to any government. Rather, the grandest, most powerful government of all human history will take complete control of survivors from among this generation.

[11] Highly favored will be those of this generation who will be privileged to see the fulfillment of what the prophet Daniel saw in vision, giving us this description thereof: "You kept on looking until a stone was cut out not by hands, and it struck the image on its feet of iron and of molded clay and crushed them. At that time the iron, the molded clay, the copper, the silver and the gold were, all together, crushed and became like the chaff from the summer threshing floor, and the wind carried them away so that no trace at all was found of them. And as for the stone that struck the image, it became a large mountain and filled the whole earth."—Daniel 2:34, 35.

[12] What does that signify? Nothing less than that God's Messianic kingdom as symbolized by the "stone" will fill the whole earth, wherever the sons of men dwell.

[13] The seat of government will be in the heavens, where the enthroned, crowned Jesus Christ sits at the right hand of God, but it will extend its superhuman power toward the earth, not now for destructive purposes, but for the perfect rulership and blessing of all the obedient inhabitants of

11. Daniel saw the pulverized "image" displaced by what?
12. What does the mountain's filling the earth signify?
13. In what way will this be a stable government, and why?

"the whole earth." This will be a stable government, immune to any overthrow by revolutionary uprisings. It "will never be brought to ruin," nor will it have a human successor. It "will not be passed on to any other people." Unlike the kingdoms of dying human rulers from Babylon of Nimrod's day onward, "it itself will stand to times indefinite," forever. (Daniel 2:44, 45) Its heavenly Ruler, the Messianic King Jesus Christ, upon whom Jehovah God has conferred immortality, will not let his government die out. He himself will live "to times indefinite" to maintain that kingdom for the full realization of God's will and for the never-ending blessing of all obedient mankind on a perfectly ruled earth.

¹⁴ And this is how God's kingdom becomes a world government. Happy are all those of this generation today who will survive to see it become such. They may become its loving, obedient subjects forever!

---

14. Who will be the happy ones from among today's generation?

CHAPTER 5

Foretelling the Time for World Rulership

L ET us now take a look at a world map and locate the lands of Iraq, Asiatic Turkey, Syria, Lebanon, Jordan and Israel. If the rulers of those lands had been living near the beginning of the sixth century before our Common Era, they would have been under the domination of the Third World Power and here is the message that they would have officially received from Babylon:

2 "Nebuchadnezzar the king, to all the peoples, national groups and languages that are dwelling in all the earth: May your peace grow great. The signs and wonders that the Most High God has performed with me, it has seemed good to me to declare. How grand his signs are, and how mighty his wonders are! His kingdom is a kingdom to time indefinite, and his rulership is for generation after generation."—Daniel 4:1-3.

3 With those far-reaching words the then king of Babylon called attention, not to his own Babylonian Empire, the Third World Power of Bible history, but to the kingdom and rulership of the Most High God. Counted from King Nebuchadnezzar's share in the destruction of the Assyrian capital Nineveh in 632 B.C.E. down to

1, 2. Around 600 B.C.E. what did Nebuchadnezzar proclaim about God?
3. How did Nebuchadnezzar's rulership compare with God's?

the overthrow of Babylon by Cyrus the Persian in 539 B.C.E., the Babylonian Empire of Nebuchadnezzar and his dynasty lasted for ninety-three years or so, less than a century. But the kingdom and rulership of the Most High God are to time indefinite, from generation to generation, that is to say, forever, to time without end. Jehovah's kingdom and rulership are more extensive, not only in point of time, but also in the area under control. Nebuchadnezzar's empire embraced only a part of southwest Asia, the Middle East and finally Egypt, but the area under control of the Most High God is universal, taking in both heaven and earth. The Most High God is the Universal Sovereign, and forever so!

⁴ India and other modern nations and tribes have their national or tribal gods, and ancient Babylon had its gods. But Nebuchadnezzar, a worshiper of the Babylonian god Marduk, was obliged to proclaim world wide that there is a Most High God, who performs signs and wonders that are great and wonderful, in proof of his real existence. Nebuchadnezzar's proclamation tells about this.

NEBUCHADNEZZAR'S DREAM OF THE MASSIVE TREE

⁵ All of us today are interested in trees. We can plant trees, but we all have to admit that trees are not a creation of man. They were here on earth thousands of years before man's arrival in 4026 B.C.E. Some trees are marvelous for both their height and their long age, like the giant sequoias in the American state of California.

---

4. Did Nebuchadnezzar thus proclaim a god higher than Marduk?
5, 6. In what aged tree stump do we now interest ourselves?

⁶ King Nebuchadnezzar tells us about a tree higher than the tallest giant sequoia, *sempervirens,* 367.8 feet (112 meters) high. What a crash there must have been when that tree was cut down! The stump and its vast root system were left in the ground. Now let us picture to ourselves that tree stump as having bands of iron and copper tightly put around it to prevent any growth from it. For forever? No, but for two thousand five hundred and twenty years. Could a stump keep alive for that long? This tree stump under question did. And, counted from the time of Nebuchadnezzar's making his proclamation about this particular tree stump, those two thousand five hundred and twenty years would end somewhere in our own twentieth century. Well, then, has that tree stump been unbanded in our time? Would that mean anything for us today? We can find out!

THE EMPEROR'S OWN ACCOUNT AS PRESERVED

⁷ Let us first find out how this tree stump came under the notice of the ruler of the Babylonian Empire, the Third World Power of Bible prophecy. In his imperial proclamation we are told: "I, Nebuchadnezzar, happened to be at ease in my house and flourishing in my palace. There was a dream that I beheld, and it began to make me afraid. And there were mental images upon my bed and visions of my head that began to frighten me. And from me an order was being put through to bring in before me all the wise men of Babylon, that they might make known to me the very interpretation of the dream." Then what?

7, 8. Why was Nebuchadnezzar obliged to tell his dream to Daniel?

⁸ "At that time the magic-practicing priests, the conjurers, the Chaldeans and the astrologers were entering; and I was saying before them what the dream was, but its interpretation they were not making known to me. And at last there came in before me Daniel, whose name is Belteshazzar according to the name of my god and in whom there is the spirit of the holy gods; and before him I said what the dream was."—Daniel 4:4-8.

⁹ Nebuchadnezzar's experience shows how vain and futile it is for national rulers and politicians in general to resort to astrologers and clairvoyants and other occultists to try to find out accurately what the future holds. Rulers do not have with them today the prophet Daniel to whom to go, but we do have the prophetic book of Daniel. From it we can learn about things that have already marked our twentieth century and what the impending future holds for this generation. Nebuchadnezzar's dream and Daniel's interpretation of it and how it was fulfilled in an illustrative way as a seal or guarantee of its prophetic value, all of this holds an interest for us now. So let us now listen as Nebuchadnezzar tells Daniel his dream of world importance. He said:

¹⁰ "Now the visions of my head upon my bed I happened to be beholding, and, look! a tree in the midst of the earth, the height of which was immense. The tree grew up and became strong, and its very height finally reached the heavens, and it was visible to the extremity of the whole earth. Its foliage was fair, and its fruit was abundant, and there was food for all on it. Under it the beast

9. In place of Daniel, what do we have to help us prophetically?
10, 11. What happened to the tree that the king saw in his dream?

of the field would seek shade, and on its boughs the birds of the heavens would dwell, and from it all flesh would feed itself.

[11] "I [King Nebuchadnezzar] continued beholding in the visions of my head upon my bed, and, look! a watcher, even a holy one, coming down from the heavens themselves. He was calling out loudly, and this is what he was saying: 'Chop the tree down, and cut off its boughs. Shake off its foliage, and scatter its fruitage. Let the beast flee from under it, and the birds from its boughs. However, leave its rootstock itself in the earth, even with a banding of iron and of copper, among the grass of the field; and with the dew of the heavens let it be wet, and with the beast let its portion be among the vegetation of the earth. Let its heart be changed from that of mankind, and let the heart of a beast be given to it, and let seven times pass over it. By the decree of watchers the thing is, and by the saying of holy ones the request is, to the intent that people living may know that the Most High is Ruler in the kingdom of mankind and that to the one whom he wants to, he gives it and he sets up over it even the lowliest one of mankind.' "—Daniel 4:10-17.

[12] According to this description of the dream as given by King Nebuchadnezzar to Daniel the tree towered over all other trees. It was visible to all the inhabitants of the earth, so that nobody was able to ignore it. It was a good tree. Although it was not called "the tree of life," it was a life-sustaining tree, for it bore fruit in abundance, enough to feed all flesh on earth. Why, then, was

12. What questions arise as to the chopping down of that tree?

it to be like the prominent tree described in Ezekiel's prophecy, chapter thirty-one, verses three through fourteen, in being cut down? How could the chopped-down tree trunk have had the "heart" of mankind and this be changed to the "heart of a beast"? How could the chopping down of the tree and the letting of its fallen trunk lie on the grassy earth for "seven times" prove that "the Most High is Ruler in the kingdom of mankind and that to the one whom he wants to, he gives it and he sets up over it even the lowliest one of mankind"? According to the angelic "watcher" or sentinel or guardian, that was the purpose of the action portrayed in the king's dream.

INTERPRETATION OF THE DREAM

¹³ Can the Most High as Supreme Ruler issue orders for a kingdom, an empire, a world power, to be chopped down like a heaven-high tree, and can he set up another king and give that one the kingship, even though he comes from the lowliest estate of mankind?

¹⁴ These were the main questions that were really set before Daniel to answer, as King Nebuchadnezzar now asked him for the interpretation of the tree dream. (Daniel 4:18) But why did Daniel get disturbed when the Most High God revealed to him the meaning of the king's dream, and why did Nebuchadnezzar have to reassure Daniel so as not to be afraid in explaining the dream? It was because, in the first place, the chopping down of the immense tree had a direct

---

13, 14. (a) What questions must be answered with regard to God as the Chopper? (b) Whom did the tall tree picture, and why?

application to Nebuchadnezzar himself. Hence Daniel wished that this portentous dream could be fulfilled just as well upon someone else, upon adversaries who hated the king. (Daniel 4:19) Daniel answers our own questions as we hear him say:

¹⁵ "The tree that you beheld, that grew great and became strong and the height of which finally reached the heavens and which was visible to all the earth, . . . it is you, O king, because you have grown great and become strong, and your grandeur has grown great and reached to the heavens, and your rulership to the extremity of the earth." —Daniel 4:20-22.

¹⁶ So that heaven-high tree stood for rulership, a worldwide rulership as invested in someone as ruler. It was this ruler that had a "heart" that could be changed from that of mankind to that of a beast. Such a change would mean a fall, a debasement, would it not? This debasement was according to the will and purpose of the Most High God, the "Ruler in the kingdom of mankind," for Daniel went on to say to Nebuchadnezzar:

¹⁷ "And because the king beheld a watcher, even a holy one, coming down from the heavens, who was also saying: 'Chop the tree down, and ruin it. However, leave its rootstock itself in the earth, but with a banding of iron and of copper, among the grass of the field, and with the dew of the heavens let it become wet, and with the beasts of the field let its portion be until seven times themselves pass over it,' this is the interpretation, O

15-17. (a) Whose heart could be changed from human to beast-like? (b) How was Nebuchadnezzar to suffer such a debasement?

king, and the decree of the Most High is that which must befall my lord the king. And you they will be driving away from men, and with the beasts of the field your dwelling will come to be, and the vegetation is what they will give even to you to eat just like bulls; and with the dew of the heavens you yourself will be getting wet, and seven times themselves will pass over you, until you know that the Most High is Ruler in the kingdom of mankind, and that to the one whom he wants to he gives it."—Daniel 4:23-25.

[18] However, after the "seven times" pass over the king in that debased condition, what? Nebuchadnezzar's dream did not directly answer this question, but Daniel's interpretation did. Showing the bright side of the dream, Daniel said to the king: "And because they said to leave the rootstock of the tree, your kingdom will be sure to you after you know that the heavens are ruling. Therefore, O king, may my counsel seem good to you, and remove your own sins by righteousness, and your iniquity by showing mercy to the poor ones. Maybe there will occur a lengthening of your prosperity."—Daniel 4:26, 27.

[19] Despite Daniel's courageous counsel, Nebuchadnezzar continued to be proud because of being the absolute monarch of the Babylonian World Power, the Third World Power of Bible prophecy. So, a lunar year later found him walking upon the roof of the royal palace at Babylon. Then, as Daniel himself tells us, "the king was answering and saying: 'Is not this Babylon the Great, that I myself have built for the royal house with the

---

18. What bright feature did Daniel impart to the dream?
19. (a) How and when did the dream begin fulfillment on the king? (b) Why was the throne reserved for him to reoccupy it?

strength of my might and for the dignity of my majesty?' While the word was yet in the king's mouth, there was a voice that fell from the heavens: 'To you it is being said, O Nebuchadnezzar the king, "The kingdom itself has gone away from you, and from mankind they are driving even you away, and with the beasts of the field your dwelling will be. Vegetation they will give even to you to eat just like bulls, and seven times themselves will pass over you, until you know that the Most High is Ruler in the kingdom of mankind, and that to the one whom he wants to he gives it." ' "—Daniel 4:28-32.

A PROPHETIC ILLUSTRATION OF THE REALITY

²⁰ What now took place was a prophetic illustration of a reality of far vaster proportions. So Nebuchadnezzar's dream began its fulfillment in the person of a man having worldwide rulership.

²¹ That is to say, the symbolic immense "tree" was chopped down and fell crashing full length to the earth. Only the tree stump, the "rootstock," was left standing, but was banded with circles of iron and copper to halt any growth upward from it for the length of the decreed "seven times." In actuality, down came the mighty Nebuchadnezzar from his imperial throne. The "Ruler in the kingdom of mankind" forced this by striking the king of Babylon with madness, changing his heart from that of a man mighty in rulership to that of a beast, a bull that feeds on vegetation out in the field. Likely King Nebuchadnezzar's court officials recalled the dream and Daniel's interpretation and feared to replace him with any-

20-22. How did the world ruler turn from human to beastlike?

body else on the throne. But the Most High God was especially the one who was reserving the imperial throne for Nebuchadnezzar to be restored to it at the end of the appointed "seven times."—Daniel 5:18-21.

²² Things progressed just as the voice that fell from the heavens had said to the boastful world ruler: "At that moment the word itself was fulfilled upon Nebuchadnezzar, and from mankind he was being driven away, and vegetation he began to eat just like bulls, and with the dew of the heavens his own body got to be wet, until his very hair grew long just like eagles' feathers and his nails like birds' claws."—Daniel 4:33; compare Acts 12:21-23.

²³ Did this degradation of King Nebuchadnezzar mean the downfall of the Babylonian Empire? Not by any means! According to the decree of the Most High God this empire was to continue on for some decades yet as the Third World Power, which now corresponded to the banded rootstock of the immense tree seen in Nebuchadnezzar's dream. The prophet Daniel continued on as servant of the demented king, he serving as "the ruler over all the jurisdictional district of Babylon and the chief prefect over all the wise men of Babylon." Also, Daniel's three Hebrew companions, Hananiah, Mishael and Azariah, continued having a part in the administration of the affairs of that jurisdictional district. (Daniel 1:11-19; 2:48, 49; 3:30) Certainly these four prominent Jewish exiles in Babylon were measuring the time of the king's illness and were awaiting the time to receive him back in sanity to his imperial

23. Why did the king's illness not mean Babylon's downfall?

throne as a Gentile monarch who had learned well the lesson that "the Most High is Ruler in the kingdom of mankind and that to the one whom he wants to, he gives it." At the end of the "seven times" this occurred.

²⁴ The king himself tells us what happened: "And at the end of the days I, Nebuchadnezzar, lifted up to the heavens my eyes, and my own understanding began to return to me; and I blessed the Most High himself, and the One living to time indefinite I praised and glorified, because his rulership is a rulership to time indefinite and his kingdom is for generation after generation. And all the inhabitants of the earth are being considered as merely nothing, and he is doing according to his own will among the army of the heavens and the inhabitants of the earth. And there exists no one that can check his hand or that can say to him, 'What have you been doing?' " —Daniel 4:34, 35.

²⁵ At that time, as far as the prophetic dream is applied to Nebuchadnezzar himself, the iron and copper bands around the rootstock of the immense tree were snapped and removed. The literal "seven times" were up, and there was due a restoration of the sane king to power. Nebuchadnezzar makes record of this, as he goes on to say: "At the same time my understanding itself began to return to me, and for the dignity of my kingdom my majesty and my brightness themselves began to return to me; and for me even my high royal officers and my grandees began eagerly searching, and I was reestablished upon my own

24. On his recovery what did the king say about the Most High?
25. So what release did the tree stump experience at that time?

kingdom, and greatness extraordinary was added to me." (Daniel 4:36) What a "sign of healing" was thus performed by the Most High God! —Daniel 4:2; Acts 4:22.

[26] It would seem highly appropriate that Daniel, Hananiah, Mishael and Azariah as "high royal officers" should be among those who searched for the restored king as a sign of their loyalty to him and of their having safeguarded his imperial interests during his mental illness. (Compare 2 Samuel 19:11-15.) These four worshipers of Jehovah God would particularly be interested in the effect of the king's humiliating experience upon him at the hands of their God. More than all others in the king's royal service, they appreciated Nebuchadnezzar's confession of the Universal Sovereignty of the Most High "Ruler," whom Nebuchadnezzar called "the King of the heavens," reigning forever. They saw how this heavenly King gave back kingship to a man who for "seven times" was "even the lowliest one of mankind" in being degraded below the human level to that of a beast of the field. (Daniel 4:17) They understood what Jehovah had been doing!

"SEVEN TIMES"

[27] Just how long were those "seven times" during which Nebuchadnezzar was mentally deranged and incapacitated for royal rulership? In the historical work entitled "Antiquities of the Jews," produced in first-century Greek by the Jew Flavius Josephus, he treats these "seven times"

26. What Hebrews likely joined the search for the king, and why?
27. The "seven times" have long been regarded as how much time?

as "seven years." (Book X, Chapter X, paragraph 6) In the following century the Greek translator of the book of Daniel, namely, Theodotion, of Pontus, Asia Minor, between the years 180 and 182 C.E., translated the Hebrew expression as "seven years" (*heptà étē*). Other Jewish commentators understand "times" here to mean "years." In fact, a number of modern translators render it this way. *The New American Bible* (Roman Catholic) reads: "Till seven years pass over him [you]." (Daniel 4:13, 20, 22, 29, *NA*) Similarly, *A New Translation* by James Moffatt and *The Complete Bible—An American Translation* read "seven years." (Also the *Good News Bible,* of 1976)

[28] So, seven Biblical lunar years would be meant, since the time decreed was from the Author of the Holy Bible, Jehovah God. Ancient inscriptions are reported as showing that there were several years in which Nebuchadnezzar did nothing. These years might well coincide with the "seven times" of his incapacitation as a mentally deranged man.

[29] Is that, however, all there is to the matter? There is no basis for doubt that Nebuchadnezzar's dream of the heaven-high tree was prophetic, it being inspired by Jehovah God. But is the dream's fulfillment limited to that ancient fulfillment on the person of one man, King Nebuchadnezzar, for him to learn a lesson regarding rulership? Is it through his personal experience that the purport of Jehovah's dealing with him is achieved, namely, "that people living may know that the Most High is Ruler in the kingdom of mankind and that to

28. In the king's case the years were of whose reckoning?
29. Was the dream's full purpose achieved in the king's case?

the one whom he wants to, he gives it and he sets up over it even the lowliest one of mankind"? (Daniel 4:17) By setting up over the kingdom of mankind "even the lowliest one of mankind" does the Most High God set up over mankind the lowest grade of rulership over mankind? Evidently not! (Daniel 4:36, 37) For the "people living" in our momentous twentieth century, Nebuchadnezzar's dream must have a further and more far-reaching fulfillment. It does!

30 Ancient facts certify the first fulfillment of the dream of the king of Babylon. How do the later facts establish the larger and complete fulfillment of that same dream? Well, Nebuchadnezzar, who for the time being back there was pictured by the massive tree, was ruler of the Babylonian Empire. So he symbolized rulership on a world scale, having worldwide recognition. Likewise, the "tree" that was illustrated by him stood for rulership on a scale grander than that held by the king of Babylon. At that time, what rulership or dominion was greater than that of Emperor Nebuchadnezzar, which stood without a rival on earth? Only the rulership of the one whom Nebuchadnezzar acknowledged to be "the Most High," "the King of the heavens." (Daniel 4:34, 37) For that reason, the heaven-high, life-sustaining tree of the dream symbolized the UNIVERSAL SOVEREIGNTY of the Most High, Jehovah God, particularly in its relationship with our earth. This Universal Sovereignty is eternal, "to time indefinite," for all generations.

31 Such a meaning attached to the "tree" raises questions in our minds, does it not? Yes. For

30. How does the tree picture Jehovah's universal sovereignty?
31. Such a meaning given to the tree raises what questions?

example, how could such a "tree" ever be chopped down? And this at the command of the Universal Sovereign, the Most High God himself? How is it set up again? God's own written Word, the Holy Bible, explains.

[32] For a long period of time Jehovah's Universal Sovereignty was represented here on earth. How? Where? When? This was by means of the kingdom that he established over his chosen people, the twelve tribes of Israel. Particularly was this so when Jehovah's anointed one, King David, was made king over all twelve tribes of Israel, after which he moved his capital city to Jerusalem, which he had captured from the pagan Jebusites. That was in 1070 B.C.E.

[33] In that same year King David had the sacred Ark of the Covenant of Jehovah brought into the city and placed in a tent pitched near his royal palace. Thus, as it were, Jehovah began to reign in Israel's capital Jerusalem, and the Israelite king was said to sit upon "Jehovah's throne." (1 Chronicles 29:23; 16:1-31) Repeatedly King David acknowledged Jehovah to be his heavenly King, the real Ruler of Israel. (Psalms 5:2; 24:7-10; 68:24; 145:1) Certainly, then, the kingdom centered at Jerusalem with David and his royal descendants sitting there on "Jehovah's throne" represented Jehovah's Universal Sovereignty with reference to our earth.—2 Chronicles 13:5, 8.

[34] Logically that expression of Jehovah's Universal Sovereignty as exercised through King David and his royal successors at Jerusalem was what was pictured by the immense tree seen in

32, 33. How did David's kingdom stand for God's sovereignty?
34. When was that symbolic tree chopped down, and how?

Nebuchadnezzar's dream. In the dream, that all-dominating tree was chopped down. True to that dream, Divine Sovereignty as exercised through the line of Davidic kings at Jerusalem was chopped down, toppled, put out of operation. When? In 607 B.C.E., when Nebuchadnezzar of Babylon brought destruction upon Jerusalem and its temple and carried off its last enthroned king, Zedekiah of David's family, into exile to die there. Jehovah himself had the symbolic tree of sovereignty chopped down, for he himself used Nebuchadnezzar as his "servant" to bring about this overthrow. Jehovah himself took the responsibility for overturning this visible expression of his sovereignty toward our earth.—Jeremiah 25:8-11, 17-29; Ezekiel 21:22-27.

[35] At that time the bands of divine restraint as pictured by the bands of iron and copper were put around the remaining rootstock of the divine sovereignty as exercised through a royal descendant of King David. No royal sprout could come forth from this rootstock for the growing again of the divine sovereignty exercised through a Davidic king. For how long was this debased appearance of Jehovah's Universal Sovereignty to continue? For "seven times," which were prophetically illustrated by the "seven years" of Nebuchadnezzar's dethronement for him to live like a beast of the field. So, how much time do "seven times" cover?

[36] A "time" or lunar "year" used in connection with Bible prophecy averaged 360 days, that is, twelve lunar months averaging 30 days each. (Compare Genesis 7:11 through 8:4.) The "seven

---

35. For what purpose was the tree stump kept in metal bands?
36. Why could the "seven times" not mean 2,520 literal days?

times" or "seven years" would therefore amount to 7 times 360 days, or 2,520 days. Are those 2,520 days to be understood literally in this case? Well, seven lunar years or 2,520 days after Jerusalem's destruction in 607 B.C.E. and the leaving of her domain in the land of Judah desolate, Jehovah's Universal Sovereignty with respect to our earth was not reestablished, was it? No! In the year 600 B.C.E. the surviving Israelites were still exiles in Babylon, Jerusalem and the land of Judah still lay desolate, and the Babylonian Empire was still the world power of the day. It was not till sixty-three years later, or in 537 B.C.E., that the exiled Israelites were given freedom by Babylon's conqueror to leave, and reoccupy their beloved homeland. But, even then, the theocratic kingdom of the house of David was not set up again at Jerusalem.

[37] The Medo-Persian Empire had now taken over world control as the Fourth World Power of Bible prophecy, and Cyrus the Great, the Persian, was emperor. So Zerubbabel, a legal and natural heir to David's throne, was made merely the governor of the Persian province of Judah. Medo-Persia corresponded with the silver breasts and arms of the metallic image seen in the inspired dream that the prophet Daniel had to recall to Nebuchadnezzar's mind and to interpret to him. (Daniel 2:31, 32, 39) According to that same dream and its interpretation, Gentile world control was to be exercised next by the copper-like Grecian World Power and then by the ironlike Roman Empire with an outgrowth therefrom in the form of the British-American Dual World Power of modern

37. What succession of world powers must precede God's kingdom?

centuries. First after that, would Jehovah's Universal Sovereignty (as pictured by the mountain) and the kingdom (pictured by the cut-out stone) interfere with the line of Gentile world powers. (Daniel 2:32-35, 44, 45) This brings us into our own twentieth century!

[38] It is very evident, therefore, that the "seven times" of 2,520 days, as measured against the world-power "image," from head to foot, must stand for something longer than the seven literal years of Nebuchadnezzar's beastlike conduct, out in the field. So each of these 2,520 days must be treated according to the Bible rule: "A day for a year, a day for a year, is what I have given you." (Ezekiel 4:6; compare Numbers 14:34.) This would mean that the "seven times" of domination of the earth by Gentile world powers without interference from God's kingdom would extend for 2,520 years from the desolating of the land of Judah (including Jerusalem) by the Babylonians. That number of years from the middle of the seventh lunar month (or Tishri 15) of 607 B.C.E. leads up to when? To Tishri 15, or October 4/5, of 1914 C.E.

[39] At that time Jehovah God the Almighty would loosen the iron and copper bands around the symbolic rootstock of Universal Sovereignty. Thus he would permit a royal "sprout" to grow up from it for the reestablishment of His Universal Sovereignty toward all the earth. (Job 14:7-9; Isaiah 11:1, 2) This took place in the birth of the "man child" government, foretold in Revelation 12:5-10 (*AV; NW*), which government was to "shepherd all the nations with an iron rod." In Nebuchad-

---

38. When would those 2,520 days, viewed symbolically, end?
39. What followed removal of the bands from the tree stump?

nezzar's dream of the world-power "image," this event was pictured by the cutting of the "stone" out of the mountain with a view to its destroying the world-power "image." (Daniel 2:34, 35) What a meaningful way that was of marking the end of the "appointed times of the nations," the end of the "times of the Gentiles," as foretold by Jesus Christ in Luke 21:24!—*NW; AV.*

⁴⁰ From then on, the royal government that was represented by ancient Jerusalem under the kingship of David's royal family was no longer to be "trampled on," "trodden down," by Gentile world powers. It was to trample them!

⁴¹ In view of all the foregoing, the Universal Governor, who knows the end from the beginning, foretold more than just Nebuchadnezzar's time for being restored to the throne of the Babylonian World Power. Jehovah God foretold, simultaneously, the time for enforcing his own world rulership by a reasserting of his rightful Universal Sovereignty toward our earth. Having determined the time for this, we are now poised for considering the Chief Agent whom the Universal Sovereign Jehovah uses in this behalf. Shall we do so?

40. What trampling by the Gentile world powers was then to cease?
41. What more than Nebuchadnezzar's restoration did God foretell?

CHAPTER 6

God's Chief Agent in the World Government

IT WAS a cursed year, it was a blessed year, that year of 1914 C.E. "Cursed," in that then World War I broke out, ushering in an Age of Violence that has steadily grown worse down till our very day. "Blessed," in that, unseen to human eyes, up in the holy heavens, a mighty government was brought forth by the Creator of heaven and earth to work for man's lasting peace.

² As announced for decades in advance by God's "ambassadors" to all nations, the "times of the Gentiles" for world domination by Gentile world powers without interference from God's kingdom ended. (2 Corinthians 5:20; Ephesians 6:20) The Gentile nations refused to recognize that fact and raged in world war for maintaining political world domination. Yet, right on time, in 1914 C.E., at the close of those "seven times" (2,520 years) of Gentile world domination, God brought forth his heavenly government, shortly to put a total end to those warmongering Gentile nations that are now mere squatters on God's "footstool," the earth. (Daniel 2:44; 4:16, 23, 25, 32; Luke 21:24; Psalm 2:1-9) In that heavenly kingdom God's Chief Agent for the world government

1. How was 1914 C.E. a blessed as well as a cursed year?
2. For what does God's Chief Agent for world government wait?

reigns, awaiting God's time for all these hostile Gentile nations to be put under his feet in ever-lasting ruin. (Psalm 110:1-6; Hebrews 10:12, 13) Then permanent peace, like a rainbow, will beautify earth.

[3] On earth, back in 1914, there was no man that could qualify as God's chief agent for a peace-bringing world government. No, not one, not even in earthly Jerusalem in the Middle East, nor in Bethlehem. In that crucial year those famous cities were in the hands of Islamic Turks, as part of the Turkish Empire, which became involved in World War I on October 30, 1914. In December of 1917 the possession of Jerusalem changed hands, when British troops under Field Marshal Allenby captured the city. In those days a British subject, the noted Jewish chemist named Chaim Weizmann, made a vital contribution to Britain's war effort. This served as an inducement for the Balfour Declaration to be issued, whereby the British government favored the establishment of a Jewish homeland in Palestine. Years later, in May of 1948, after warfare between Arabs and Jews, the Republic of Israel was set up. The distinguished Chaim Weizmann became its first president, but not its Davidic king. He did not qualify as God's Chief Agent.

[4] Kingdoms were destroyed as a result of World War I. In accord with this destructive trend, no new kingdom was born on earth in 1914, at the end of the "appointed times of the nations," or, "the times of the Gentiles." Later, the League of Nations assigned to Britain a mandate over

3. In 1914 or later did any human qualify to be World Governor?
4. Why was no new kingdom born at Jerusalem in 1914 C.E.?

Jerusalem and Middle Eastern territories captured by British troops. This mandate expired on May 15, 1948. The Republic of Israel followed. Still, no visible kingdom of God had been established on earth to serve as an agency of Jehovah's universal sovereignty toward our earth. No man of Jewish stock had been found to qualify as His Chief Agent in His promised world government. There was no circumcised Jew that could produce valid credentials proving that he was a real descendant of King David, with either a natural right or a legal right to King David's throne at Jerusalem.

[5] So where, at the crucial time, was the true heir of King David to be found, the needed one whom Jehovah could install as his Chief Agent in the foretold world government? Under the circumstances, to what other place could we possibly look than up in the invisible spirit realm, the heavens where the Universal Sovereign himself reigns? That is where the ancient prophet Daniel pointed for the presentation of Jehovah's Chief Agent. That is where the search must be made for the divinely approved, qualified individual. There, also, is where the Galilean John the son of Zebedee, in the last book of the Bible, Revelation, revealed that a search *would* be made for a worthy individual to perform the duties of Jehovah's Chief Agent.—Revelation 5:3-12.

[6] Let us now, with the eye of prophecy, look heavenward with the prophet Daniel and observe his portrayal of the greatly desired Chief Agent. Daniel shows that it was near the end of the long

---

5. Where then did search have to be made for God's Chief Agent?
6, 7. What three beasts did Daniel first see in a vision?

exile of the Jews in Babylon when God favored him with the vision about His Chief Agent. Daniel dates the vision as he writes: "In the first year of Belshazzar [Nebuchadnezzar's grandson] the king of Babylon, Daniel himself beheld a dream and visions of his head upon his bed. At that time he wrote down the dream itself. The complete account of the matters he told. Daniel was speaking up and saying:

⁷ " 'I happened to be beholding in my visions during the night, and, see there! the four winds of the heavens were stirring up the vast sea. And four huge beasts were coming up out of the sea, each one being different from the others. The first one was like a lion, and it had the wings of an eagle. I kept on beholding until its wings were plucked out, and it was lifted up from the earth and was made to stand up on two feet just like a man, and there was given to it the heart of a man. And, see there! another beast, a second one, it being like a bear. And on one side it was raised up, and there were three ribs in its mouth between its teeth; and this is what they were saying to it, "Get up, eat much flesh." After this I kept on beholding, and, see there! another beast, one like a leopard, but it had four wings of a flying creature on its back. And the beast had four heads, and there was given to it rulership indeed.' "—Daniel 7:1-6.

⁸ Those three huge beasts out of the windswept sea pictured three rulerships. They pictured the same rulerships as represented in the gold head, the silver breasts and arms, the copper belly and thighs of Nebuchadnezzar's dream image, namely,

---

8. What did those three beasts symbolize, for how long?

the Babylonian World Power, the Medo-Persian World Power and the Grecian World Power. These world powers occupied that period of the "times of the Gentiles" from the desolating of Jerusalem and the land of Judah in 607 B.C.E. and down to 30 B.C.E. In that year the last one of the four Hellenic kingdoms that resulted from the Grecian Empire of Alexander the Great suffered decisive defeat by the naval forces of ancient pagan Rome.

⁹ At this point, however, Daniel is not finished with telling us his prophetic dream. He adds: "After this I kept on beholding in the visions of the night, and, see there! a fourth beast, fearsome and terrible and unusually strong. And it had teeth of iron, big ones. It was devouring and crushing, and what was left it was treading down with its feet. And it was something different from all the other beasts that were prior to it, and it had ten horns. I kept on considering the horns, and, look! another horn, a small one, came up in among them, and there were three of the first horns that were plucked up from before it. And, look! there were eyes like the eyes of a man in this horn, and there was a mouth speaking grandiose things."—Daniel 7:7, 8.

¹⁰ Here we have what corresponds with the iron legs of the world-power "image" seen in Nebuchadnezzar's dream. The fourth beast represented more than just the Roman Empire or Sixth World Power of Bible prophecy. We learn this from the conversation that Daniel had with the angelic interpreter, who told Daniel: "As for these huge beasts, because they are four, there are four kings that will stand up from the earth.

9. What fourth beast with horns did Daniel see in this vision?
10. This beast corresponds with what in the dream "image"?

But the holy ones of the Supreme One will receive the kingdom, and they will take possession of the kingdom for time indefinite, even for time indefinite upon times indefinite." (Daniel 7:17, 18) Despite this information, there still remained a mystery for Daniel regarding the fourth beast.

¹¹ "Then it was that I desired to make certain concerning the fourth beast, . . . and concerning the ten horns that were on its head, and the other horn that came up and before which three fell, even that horn that had eyes and a mouth speaking grandiose things and the appearance of which was bigger than that of its fellows. I kept on beholding when that very horn made war upon the holy ones, and it was prevailing against them, until the Ancient of Days came and judgment itself was given in favor of the holy ones of the Supreme One, and the definite time arrived that the holy ones took possession of the kingdom itself."—Daniel 7:19-22.

¹² Like Daniel, we today would like to know what that little horn that had eyes and a mouth pictured. We ought to arrive at its meaning under the guidance of God's holy spirit, especially so since we have lived to see the fulfillment of the prophetic dream of Daniel. Accordingly, we now do well to listen to what the angelic interpreter said to Daniel in explanation:

¹³ "This is what he said, 'As for the fourth beast, there is a fourth kingdom that will come to be on the earth, that will be different from all the other kingdoms; and it will devour all the earth and will trample it down and crush it. And as for the ten horns, out of that [fourth]

11. What additional feature of it did Daniel want explained?
12, 13. How did the angel explain the small horn for us?

kingdom there are ten kings that will rise up; and still another one will rise up after them, and he himself will be different from the first ones, and three kings he will humiliate. And he will speak even words against the Most High, and he will harass continually the holy ones themselves of the Supreme One. And he will intend to change times and law, and they will be given into his hand for a time, and times and half a time. And the Court itself proceeded to sit, and his own rulership they finally took away, in order to annihilate him and to destroy him totally.'" —Daniel 7:23-26.

14 In verse twenty-five where the expression "a time, and times and half a time" appears, *The New American Bible* (Roman Catholic) reads: "They [the holy ones] shall be handed over to him for a year, two years, and a half-year." Moffatt's translation reads: "And for three years and half a year the saints shall be handed over to him." Similarly, *The Complete Bible—An American Translation* reads: "And they shall be handed over to him for a year, two years, and half a year." Historically, what years were they?

THE ANGLO-AMERICAN DUAL WORLD POWER

15 The "fourth kingdom," the Roman Empire, broke up into a number of nations, and one outstanding outgrowth from the empire was Great Britain. To establish itself as the mistress of the seven seas Great Britain with its colonies had to prove itself superior to the Spanish, the Dutch and the French naval powers. This was accomplished by the year 1763 C.E., so that then the

---

14. The "time, and times and half a time" are how long?
15. How did the "small" horn with eyes and mouth come to be?

British Empire became the foretold Seventh World Power of Bible prophecy. On July 4, 1776, the former British colonies in North America declared their independence and became the United States of America. By later cooperation together in various fields of international importance the British Empire and the United States of America became, in effect, the Anglo-American Dual World Power. Down to 1914 C.E. this Seventh World Power controlled more than a quarter of the earth's surface and population. It is the "small" horn that plucked up three other horns (Spanish, Dutch and French naval powers) and that had the eyes of a man and a mouth speaking grandiose things.—Daniel 7:8.

16 It was during World War I, from July 28, 1914, to November 11, 1918, that the "saints" or "holy ones" were handed over to this Seventh World Power to do with as it wanted. It was on April 6, 1917, that the United States of America became involved in that world conflict on the side of the British Empire. Daniel's prophecy specializes on three and a half lunar years during this World War I as the time when the Seventh World Power, the symbolic "small" horn, crushed the "holy ones" of the Most High God, Jehovah. This culminated in the sentencing to many years of imprisonment in the federal penitentiary at Atlanta, Georgia, of seven falsely accused Christian men who were engaged prominently in publishing world wide the good news of God's established kingdom by word of mouth and by printed page.

17 This sentencing occurred on June 21, 1918, and on July 4, 1918, these seven leading promoters

16, 17. How did those three and a half years culminate in 1918?

of Bible study were taken by train from Brooklyn, New York, to Atlanta, Georgia. This served as a crushing spiritual blow to the then-persecuted International Bible Students, who, now, since the year 1931, are known as Jehovah's Witnesses.

18 Daniel's prophecy does not show that the "holy ones themselves of the Supreme One" were wiped out by harassment from the symbolic "small" horn, the Anglo-American Dual World Power. The Most High God, whose universal sovereignty they stick to and proclaim, is on their side. He will see to it that divine justice is done to them. (Luke 18:7, 8) However, the Seventh World Power and all the other nations of the earth do not take seriously the notice served on them by Jehovah's Witnesses. This notice is to the effect that, since the end of the Gentile Times in 1914, they have been on judgment before the Most High. Daniel's dream of the four beasts and the "small" horn prophetically portrays this solemn fact.

THE DIVINE COURT SITS

19 Referring to a time after the "small" horn has come into existence and has spoken grandiose things, Daniel continues on with describing his prophetic dream: "I kept on beholding until there were thrones placed and the Ancient of Days sat down. His clothing was white just like snow, and the hair of his head was like clean wool. His throne was flames of fire; its wheels were a burning fire. There was a stream of fire flowing and going out from before him. There

---

18. Are the "holy ones" shown as wiped out by the "small" horn?
19. How did the Heavenly Court deal with the four "beasts"?

were a thousand thousands that kept ministering to him, and ten thousand times ten thousand that kept standing right before him. The Court took its seat, and there were books that were opened. I kept on beholding at that time because of the sound of the grandiose words that the horn was speaking; I kept on beholding until the [fourth] beast was killed and its body was destroyed and it was given to the burning fire. But as for the rest of the beasts, their rulerships were taken away, and there was a lengthening in life given to them for a time and a season."—Daniel 7:9-12.

[20] It is only here in this vision to Daniel that the immortal God who is without beginning is called "the Ancient of Days." He has priority over everyone and everything else, he being their Creator. (Psalm 90:2) As the all-wise, all-righteous One who preceded all his creations, he rightly sits as the Judge of all things, our earth included. Since his days extend into the ancient past, he knows all past human history as if it were written in a book. Thus he has observed all four of those beastlike world powers in their course of action. He passes judgment upon them, not on the basis of what others testify, but according to what he knows about them directly. He does not have to consult a written record, containing accounts written by angels. In earthly human courts, lawbooks and reference books would have to be consulted. But not so with Jehovah, "the Ancient of Days."

[21] As history books show, the four imperial "beasts" passed off the worldly scene one after the other, in the order of the four metals seen in

20. Why does "the Ancient of Days" need no books to consult?
21. How were the lives of the "rest of the beasts" lengthened?

Nebuchadnezzar's dream of the world-power image. First the Babylonian World Power made its exit off the stage, after it the Medo-Persian World Power, then the Grecian World Power, and finally the Roman World Power. Although those world powers lost their rulership one after the other, their imperial territories and the inhabitants thereof continued on, some remnants of these existing down to this day. That is why Daniel 7:12 says: "But as for the rest of the beasts, their rulerships were taken away, and there was a lengthening in life given to them for a time and a season."

²² The fourth symbolic "beast," with its aggressive "small" horn, suffers destruction because of its violent oppressive course on earth, because of its blasphemous words against the Most High God, and because of its continual harassment of God's "holy ones." Such ungodly things have been done more recently by the Anglo-American horn on the head of this fourth beast.

²³ So, the symbolic fourth beast is pictured as being destroyed along with the "small" horn. In historical reality, however, the symbolic fourth beast, namely, the Roman World Power, has its imperial power taken away, in order to make room for the Anglo-American Dual World Power. Various "kings," or symbolic "horns," that had been embraced within the Roman World Power, continued on ruling like inferior "horns," dominated by the crafty "small" horn that had a man's eyes and a talkative mouth. So, when the Anglo-American Dual World Power goes down into destruction under the fiery judgments of the

---

22. Why is the fourth beast with its "small" horn destroyed?
23. What happens to rulerships not pictured by the four beasts?

Ancient of Days, those hornlike "kings," as remnants of the Roman World Power, perish with it. (Daniel 7:23-26) But how about those empires, kingdoms, republics and political bodies that were never a part of the Roman Empire or of the Anglo-American Dual World Power, including the British Commonwealth of Nations? All these, too, must be destroyed when the Ancient of Days executes fiery judgment on this world.—Revelation 16:13 through 19:21.

GOD'S CHIEF AGENT IS INTRODUCED

²⁴ Will such destruction of all earthly human governments and rulerships leave human affairs in a chaotic state, subject to anarchy, lawlessness, and ungoverned? Let us not be afraid of the fast-approaching fiery destruction of this worldly system of things. The Supreme Judge, the Ancient of Days, is in charge of our earth. He must do away with the man-made political governments of misrule and oppression in order to make room for the finest government that mankind could ever have. It will be an expression of his own Universal Sovereignty toward mankind's earthly home. It will be an indivisible World Government that will exercise its power and authority from heaven, a location superior to London, Washington, Moscow, Peking, Tokyo, or any other national capital on earth. Jehovah introduces to us his Chief Agent in that World Government in the prophetic dream that he inspired Daniel to have. Daniel points heavenward as he now writes:

²⁵ "I kept on beholding in the visions of the night, and, see there! with the clouds of the

24. Does destruction of human rule leave earth ungoverned?
25. How is God's Chief Agent introduced in Daniel 7:13, 14?

heavens someone like a son of man happened to be coming; and to the Ancient of Days he gained access, and they brought him up close even before that One. And to him there were given rulership and dignity and kingdom, that the peoples, national groups and languages should all serve even him. His rulership is an indefinitely lasting rulership that will not pass away, and his kingdom one that will not be brought to ruin." —Daniel 7:13, 14.

[26] Who is that "someone like a son of man" that comes, not up from the earth, but from the heavens "with the clouds" and gains access to the Ancient of Days enthroned in the judicial court? Some think that, because this "someone like a son of man" is not mentioned thereafter in the prophecy but the "holy ones of the Supreme One" are spoken of as getting kingdom rulership, it refers to a composite person, God's "holy nation" as a body. But there is a reliable authority who points out who that "someone like a son of man" really is. How so?

[27] Over nineteen hundred years ago, on Passover night (Nisan 14) of the year 33 C.E., a natural descendant of King David stood on trial for his life before the judicial Sanhedrin of Jerusalem. After this man refused to answer to the accusing testimonies that were offered against him, the presiding high priest said to him: "By the living God I put you under oath to tell us whether you are the Christ the Son of God!" Did the accused man now recognize himself to be under oath before the living God to tell the truth about him-

---

26. Some men argue that "someone like a son of man" pictures whom?

27, 28. (a) How was an authority obliged to identify who that "someone like a son of man" is? (b) How was he then treated?

self? Yes! He recognized the high priest's judicial authority to put him under oath to state the facts, even though he knew that his telling the truth would make him appear as a shocking blasphemer to the Supreme Sanhedrin.

[28] The record of the court trial tells us: "Jesus said to him: 'You yourself said it. Yet I say to you men, From henceforth you will see the Son of man sitting at the right hand of power and coming on the clouds of heaven.' Then the high priest ripped his outer garments, saying: 'He has blasphemed! What further need do we have of witnesses? See! Now you have heard the blasphemy. What is your opinion?' They returned answer: 'He is liable to death.' Then they spit into his face and hit him with their fists. Others slapped him in the face, saying: 'Prophesy to us, you Christ. Who is it that struck you?' "—Matthew 26:63-68.

[29] There, then, was the one man on earth who could reliably refer to Daniel's prophecy, chapter seven, verse thirteen, and correctly identify who that "someone like a son of man" really was. Sixty-three years later Jesus Christ, resurrected from the dead and glorified in heaven, transmitted a revelation to his apostle John on earth, and John was inspired to write concerning him: "Look! He is coming with the clouds, and every eye will see him, and those who pierced him; and all the tribes of the earth will beat themselves in grief because of him. Yes, Amen." (Revelation 1:7) This as well as other statements of the Bible prove that the "someone like a son of man" as seen in Daniel's vision is Jesus Christ

---

29. What else shows that Daniel 7:13 does not mean a composite body?

the Descendant of King David. In Psalm 8:4 (*AV*) David spoke prophetically of him as "the son of man." (Hebrews 2:5-8, *AV*) Repeatedly Jesus spoke of himself as "the Son of man." Not the company of "the holy ones themselves of the Supreme One," but David's royal Descendant is the individual pictured in Daniel 7:13 as coming "with the clouds of the heavens."—Matthew 24:30.

³⁰ When does this particular coming take place? According to the verses preceding Daniel 7:13 it was to take place after the "small" horn that plucks up three other horns on the head of the fourth beast grew up, which was in the latter half of the eighteenth century C.E. Hence the Son of man's coming "with the clouds of the heavens" was not before then, not even in 70 C.E., when his prophecy came true: "They [the rebellious Jews] shall fall by the edge of the sword, and shall be led away captive into all nations: and Jerusalem shall be trodden down of the Gentiles [the non-Jewish nations], until the times of the Gentiles be fulfilled." (Luke 21:24, *AV*) Those "times of the Gentiles" had begun at the desolation of Jerusalem by the Babylonians in 607 B.C.E. During those Gentile Times the non-Jewish nations were permitted to dominate the earth without interference from God's Davidic kingdom.

³¹ At the close of those Gentile Times, in 1914 C.E., David's royal Heir could rightfully apply to God for Kingdom rule.

³² Events in fulfillment of Bible prophecies from 1914 C.E. down till now prove that the Son of

---

30, 31. Daniel 7:13 was fulfilled, but why not in 70 C.E.?
32, 33. Why did we not see the coming of the one with legal right?

man's coming occurred in that year. Of course, none of us saw such a coming with our literal eyes. We could not have done so, for Daniel 7:13, 14 describes the Son of man as coming, not to earth, but to the Ancient of Days, the Judge in heaven who "is changing times and seasons, removing kings and setting up kings." (Daniel 2:21) He came at the invitation of the Ancient of Days, as recorded in Psalm 2:8, 9: "Ask of me, that I may give nations as your inheritance and the ends of the earth as your own possession. You will break them with an iron scepter, as though a potter's vessel you will dash them to pieces." Then without running ahead of his judicial time schedule the Ancient of Days could do what he foretold at Ezekiel 21:25-27. There, after commanding the removal of the turban and crown of Davidic kingship, he said:

[33] "Put on high even what is low, and bring low even the high one [the occupant of King David's throne]. A ruin, a ruin, a ruin I shall make it. As for this also, it will certainly become no one's until he comes who has the legal right, and I must give it to him."

[34] All the evidence to date is that the Ancient of Days did give to the Davidic Heir with the "legal right" the Messianic kingdom at the end of the Gentile Times in 1914. As Daniel 7:14 foretold: "To him there were given rulership and dignity and kingdom, that the peoples, national groups and languages should all serve even him. His rulership is an indefinitely lasting rulership that will not pass away, and his kingdom one that will not be brought to ruin." That was the pre-

34. So how did God display universal sovereignty in 1914?

cise time for the symbolic bands of iron and copper to be removed from around the "rootstock" of Divine Universal Sovereignty now that the prophetic "seven times" of 2,520 years had ended. It was then the marked time for Jehovah's Universal Sovereignty to assert itself toward our earth once again. How? By having a "sprout" grow up out of that long-dormant "rootstock," and thereby prove that "the Most High is Ruler in the kingdom of mankind and that to the one whom he wants to, he gives it and he sets up over it even the lowliest one of mankind."—Daniel 4:17, 23, 32; Isaiah 11:1; Zechariah 3:8; 6:12.

[35] That, too, was the time for the symbolic "stone" to be cut out of the "mountain" of God's Universal Sovereignty and then to be hurled against the "image" of political world power on earth. It is aimed to strike the "feet" of iron and molded clay. Then it must grind the whole idolatrous image to powder. Finally it must grow into a mountain, to fill all the earth.—Daniel 2:34, 45.

[36] Correspondingly, in 1914 the Messianic kingdom came forth from the womb of Jehovah's wifelike organization in heaven, and the words of Revelation 12:5 came true: "She gave birth to a son, a male, who is to shepherd all the nations with an iron rod. And her child was caught away to God and to his throne." Then, doubtless, it was that the thousand thousands of angels who ministered to the Ancient of Days and the ten thousand times ten thousand who stand right before him joined their voices in announcing universe wide: "The kingdom of the world did become the

---

35. What royal "stone" was then put in motion, against what?
36. What royal birth then occurred, and also what announcement?

kingdom of our Lord and of his Christ, and he will rule as king forever and ever."—Revelation 11:15; Daniel 7:10.

[37] In the light of all the above, who, then, is God's Chief Agent for our incoming world government? Jesus Christ, the now glorified Permanent Heir of King David. As a perfect man in David's royal line, he "offered one sacrifice for sins perpetually and sat down at the right hand of God [in 33 C.E.], from then on awaiting until his enemies should be placed as a stool for his feet." —Hebrews 10:12, 13; 1:3, 4; Psalm 110:1-6.

[38] In the coming world rule there will be sharers with God's Chief Agent, for Daniel 7:27, 28 declares: " 'And the kingdom and the rulership and the grandeur of the kingdoms under all the heavens were given to the people who are the holy ones of the Supreme One. Their kingdom is an indefinitely lasting kingdom, and all the rulerships will serve and obey even them.' Up to this point is the end of the matter." So now the question arises, Were the "people who are the holy ones of the Supreme One" the prophet Daniel's own fleshly people, the nation of natural, circumcised Jews or Israelites? Were the twelve tribes of Israel who were the flesh-and-blood descendants of Abraham, Isaac and Jacob to become the top-ranking people during the indefinitely lasting reign of the Messiah (Christ), with all the Gentile nations to become subject to them as world rulers? People of all races have asked this question. Shall we now consider it together?

37. Who, therefore, must God's Chief Agent in rulership be?
38. What questions arise about the "holy ones" who share in ruling?

CHAPTER 7

The Picking Out of Sharers in the World Rule

WHO will be the sharers with the glorified Permanent Heir of King David in the promised World Government? How many sharers will there be? And where—here on earth, or up in heaven? Once such questions were a mystery. But no more!

² Toward the end of the first century of our Common Era, King David's Permanent Heir in the Messianic kingdom, namely, Jesus Christ, disclosed the desired answers. By a miraculous revelation he transmitted from heaven the information to a man here on earth, not at Jerusalem, but on the prison island of Patmos in the Aegean Sea, not far from ancient Ephesus, Asia Minor. Yes, that man was a natural, circumcised Jew. Was that Jew there on that Roman penal island because he had joined the Jewish revolt, in the year 66 C.E., that led to the nation's destruction by the Roman legions in 70 C.E.? Well, let us have this Jewish prisoner tell us:

³ "I John, your brother and a sharer with you in the tribulation and kingdom and endurance in company with Jesus, came to be in the isle that is called Patmos for [what?] speaking about God and bearing witness to Jesus. By inspiration

---

1. What points about sharers in world rule were once a mystery?
2, 3. Where was John on receiving the Revelation, and why?

I came to be in the Lord's day, and I heard behind me a strong voice like that of a trumpet, saying: 'What you see write in a scroll and send it to the seven congregations, in Ephesus and in Smyrna and in Pergamum and in Thyatira and in Sardis and in Philadelphia and in Laodicea.'" —Revelation 1:9-11.

⁴ This John, the son of Zebedee, had been a fisherman in the Sea of Galilee, but had left his fishing profession to become a 'fisher of men,' one of the twelve apostles of the Messiah Jesus. (Matthew 4:18-22; Luke 5:1-11) So John was a Christianized Jew, a faithful disciple of Jesus as the Messiah, the Christ, the one "anointed" with God's spirit to be the Messianic King. John had been an eyewitness of the impalement of this Jesus Christ at Calvary, and on the third day thereafter he had seen the resurrected Jesus. On the fortieth day thereafter he and his fellow apostles had seen the resurrected Jesus Christ ascend to heaven, to sit down at the right hand of God, his heavenly Father.

⁵ Furthermore, John the apostle was there in Jerusalem on the day of Pentecost of 33 C.E., when Jehovah God used Jesus as his Chief Agent in pouring out holy spirit upon about one hundred and twenty assembled disciples. (Acts 1:1 through 2:36) So by the time that John wrote down the Revelation in 96 C.E., he had endured tribulation and suffering as a Christian for sixty-three years. John spoke of himself as a "sharer" in the kingdom with his fellow disciples of Christ. How many sharers were there to be in that Kingdom world

---

4, 5. (a) How had John come into relationship with Jesus Christ? (b) In what was John then a sharer with those to whom he wrote?

government? John refers to himself as "the disciple whom Jesus used to love," and he was favored with this information.—John 13:23; 21:20.

⁶ The apostle John could remember how, back in 29 C.E., John the Baptizer pointed to the spirit-anointed Jesus and said: "See, the Lamb of God!" And John the son of Zebedee followed Jesus for this reason. (John 1:36-39) Consequently, sixty-seven years afterward, when John saw and heard in an inspired vision the glorified Jesus Christ spoken of as "the Lamb," he understood who was meant—no one else but Jesus Christ, who, on earth, had been sacrificed like an innocent lamb on God's altar. (John 1:29; 1 Peter 1:18, 19) Many times during the years 30-33 C.E., John had stood with this symbolic Lamb, Jesus Christ, on the earthly Mount Zion, the mountain on which the original Jerusalem had stood. But that earthly mountain became used as a symbol of a site in heaven where the Messianic world government would have its seat. Who will stand there as sharers with the Lamb Jesus Christ in the heavenly world government? John observed the number and said:

⁷ "And I saw, and, look! the Lamb standing upon the Mount Zion, and with him a hundred and forty-four thousand having his name and the name of his Father written on their foreheads. And they are singing as if a new song before the throne and before the four living creatures and the elders; and no one was able to master that song but the hundred and forty-four thousand,

6, 7. (a) On what mountain had John often stood with the Lamb Jesus Christ? (b) How many did John see standing with Him on the heavenly Mount Zion?

who have been bought from the earth. These are the ones that did not defile themselves with women; in fact, they are virgins. These are the ones that keep following the Lamb no matter where he goes. These were bought from among mankind as firstfruits to God and to the Lamb, and no falsehood was found in their mouths; they are without blemish."—Revelation 14:1, 3-5.

8 Ah, then, just one hundred and forty-four thousand were "bought from the earth," "bought from among mankind as firstfruits to God and to the Lamb," for a place on the governmental Mount Zion in the heavens. What? Only 144,000 from among the billions of people that have lived and died during the past nineteen centuries since the days of Christ's apostles? So few comparatively as 144,000? How different this Scriptural fact is from the idea in Christendom that the hundreds of millions of her church members will go to heaven at death! Here let us remember that "firstfruits" of any harvest are not the whole crop, but are merely a small token selection from the whole crop. Jesus hinted at the fewness of the Kingdom members when he said to his disciples: "Have no fear, *little* flock, because your Father has approved of giving you the kingdom. Sell the things belonging to you and give gifts of mercy. Make purses for yourselves that do not wear out, a never-failing treasure in the heavens." —Luke 12:32, 33.

SPIRITUAL ISRAELITES

9 That comparatively small number, 144,000, is not a miscalculation. It was also set forth earlier

---

8. What indicated there would be a fewness of Kingdom sharers?
9, 10. (a) With what did the 144,000 have to be sealed? (b) Out of what nation were they sealed, and how many to a division?

by John, in Revelation 7:1-8. It is there made clear that one of the requirements for being one of the "little flock" of Kingdom sharers is that of being marked in the forehead with the identifying "seal of the living God," besides having written on the forehead, as it were, the name of the Lamb and the name of his Father, Jehovah God. How many meet this requirement, and of what nation or race are they? The apostle John leaves us in no doubt about this, saying:

[10] "And I heard the number of those who were sealed, a hundred and forty-four thousand, sealed out of every tribe of the sons of Israel: Out of the tribe of Judah twelve thousand sealed; out of the tribe of Reuben twelve thousand; out of the tribe of Gad twelve thousand; out of the tribe of Asher twelve thousand; out of the tribe of Naphtali twelve thousand; out of the tribe of Manasseh twelve thousand; out of the tribe of Simeon twelve thousand; out of the tribe of Levi twelve thousand; out of the tribe of Issachar twelve thousand; out of the tribe of Zebulun twelve thousand; out of the tribe of Joseph twelve thousand; out of the tribe of Benjamin twelve thousand sealed."—Revelation 7:4-8.

[11] The names of these twelve tribes differ from the list of names of the original twelve tribes of natural Israel, as given in Genesis 49:3-28. Rightly so, for Revelation 7:4-8 presents the names of the tribes of *spiritual* Israel. They have to be spiritual Israelites if they are to stand with the Lamb Jesus Christ on the heavenly Mount Zion.

11, 12. (a) Of what kind of Israel do the 144,000 have to be? (b) According to Romans 9:29 and 11:5, how many natural Jews qualified?

(Revelation 14:1-3; Hebrews 12:22) Here we have to take into consideration the words addressed to the Lamb Jesus Christ, at Revelation 5:9, 10: "You were slaughtered and with your blood you bought persons for God out of [whom? Out of natural, circumcised Israel? No, but out of] every tribe and tongue and people and nation, and you made them to be a kingdom and priests to our God, and they are to rule as kings over the earth." Bible history shows that there were only a "remnant" of Jews according to the flesh that became Christians. It was just as the Christianized Jew, the apostle Paul, said:

[12] "Unless Jehovah of armies had left a seed to us, we should have become just like Sodom, and we should have been made just like Gomorrah." Also: "In this way, therefore, at the present season also a remnant has turned up according to a choosing due to undeserved kindness [and not according to fleshly Israelite descent]." —Romans 9:29; 11:5.

[13] In order for 144,000 persons "out of every tribe and tongue and people and nation" to be rated as "Israelites" they would have to be such in a figurative sense, that is, be *inwardly* Israelites. As Romans 2:29 reminds us: "He is a Jew who is one on the inside, and his circumcision is that of the heart by spirit."

[14] Moreover, another indispensable thing calls for the sharers with Jesus Christ in the world rule to be Israelites of a spiritual kind. This indispensable feature is what Jesus called to the attention of the Jewish ruler Nicodemus, saying:

13, 14. (a) Do the 144,000 need to be fleshly Israelites? (b) To what extent do they have to be spiritual Israelites?

"Unless anyone is born again, he cannot see the kingdom of God. . . . Unless anyone is born from water and spirit, he cannot enter into the kingdom of God. What has been born from the flesh is flesh, and what has been born from the spirit is spirit. . . . So is everyone that has been born from the spirit." (John 3:3-8) Accordingly, the natural Jews as well as the non-Jews who become the dedicated, baptized disciples of Christ and whom God picks out to share with Christ in world rule God begets with his spirit. All such become spiritual Israelites.

[15] We can therefore appreciate that such spirit-begotten Christians (drawn from both Jews and Gentiles) are a "new creation." These conduct themselves according to this divine "rule," and not according to the Law code given through Moses at Mount Sinai, Arabia. It is with respect to those belonging to this "new creation" that the Christianized Jew Paul writes: "All those who will walk orderly by this rule of conduct, upon them be peace and mercy, even upon the Israel of God."—Galatians 6:15, 16.

[16] Consequently, it is wrong, unscriptural, for anyone to argue that the natural, circumcised Jews, "that which is Israel in a fleshly way," are going to become the world rulers on earth with Jerusalem of the Republic of Israel as their capital. (1 Corinthians 10:18) People who now belong to Gentile nations will not come under any world rule of such natural, circumcised Israelites. Rather, all nationalities, including the fleshly Jews, will come under the world rule of the heavenly

---

15. Who now make up the "Israel of God"?
16. Will Gentiles come under rule by a Jew at earthly Jerusalem?

"twelve tribes" of spiritual Israel, along with its King Jesus Christ, at God's due time, shortly.

RESURRECTION TO RULERSHIP
IN THE WORLD GOVERNMENT

[17] Jehovah God, the Universal Sovereign, predestinated or foreordained the number that would share with Christ in the Kingdom rule over all the earth. He also foreordained the requirements and personal qualifications for those worthy to share in the world rule. That is why there will be only 144,000 who share with Jesus Christ in the world government. They must be spiritual Israelites. Aside from his Son Jesus Christ, Jehovah did not predestine or foreordain individuals. Rather, he set out in advance the requirements and personal qualifications for Kingdom heirs. In the light of this we understand Romans 8:29, 30:

[18] "Those whom he gave his first recognition he also foreordained to be patterned after the image of his Son, that he might be the firstborn among many brothers. Moreover, those whom he foreordained are the ones he also called; and those whom he called are the ones he also declared to be righteous [or, whom he justified]. Finally those whom he declared righteous are the ones he also glorified."

[19] According to foreordained requirements, those who are "patterned after the image" of the Son of God must suffer with him now, just as the apostle John on the isle of Patmos indicated. They are required to endure even to the death. But for their comfort the apostle Paul wrote: "Faithful is the saying: Certainly if we died

---

17, 18. What did God foreordain about sharers in world rule?
19. What sufferings are foreordained for sharers in world rule?

together, we shall also live together; if we go on enduring, we shall also rule together as kings." (2 Timothy 2:11, 12) And the prisoner apostle John was instructed to write the congregation at Smyrna: "Do not be afraid of the things you are about to suffer. Look! The Devil will keep on throwing some of you into prison that you may be fully put to the test, and that you may have tribulation ten days. Prove yourself faithful even to death, and I will give you the crown of life." —Revelation 2:10.

[20] Since the 144,000 spiritual Israelites are those "who have been bought from the earth" and "bought from among mankind," their future is no longer on earth and among mankind. As "first-fruits to God and to the Lamb," they must be presented to these ones in heaven. So their resurrection out of death, down to which they have proved faithful, has to be to spirit life in heaven. Theirs is the spiritual resurrection that is described in 1 Corinthians 15:42-55. (Revelation 14:3, 4) For suffering in association with Christ and proving faithful to God even to the death, the 144,000 spiritual Israelites are most highly rewarded by the God who can resurrect the dead. The reward held out to these faithful ones is envisioned for us in Revelation 20:4-6. There the apostle John, who himself expected the heavenly reward, writes:

[21] "And I saw thrones, and there were those who sat down on them, and power of judging was given them. Yes, I saw the souls of those executed with the ax [why?] for the witness they bore to Jesus and for speaking about God, and those who

20, 21. What kind of resurrection does theirs have to be? Why?

had worshiped neither the wild beast nor its image and who had not received the mark upon their forehead and upon their hand. And they came to life and ruled as kings with the Christ for a thousand years. . . . This is the first resurrection. Happy and holy is anyone having part in the first resurrection; over these the second death has no authority, but they will be priests of God and of the Christ, and will rule as kings with him for the thousand years."

[22] From the first century C.E. onward till now, the 144,000 spiritual Israelites, who are selected for the heavenly rule as kings with Jesus Christ, have refused to worship the symbolic "wild beast," that is, the political organization for rulership of all the earth by means of human governments. During the lifetime of the spiritual Israelites from apostolic days till now the Roman World Power and the Anglo-American Dual World Power have been the dominant members of the political "wild beast," like the last two "heads" on this seven-headed wild beast.

[23] The Anglo-American Dual World Power, the Seventh World Power of Bible prophecy, has been the chief one to propose and to maintain the "image" of the "wild beast." This "image" of global rule by man-made governments was, first, the League of Nations, and, now, is the United Nations, for keeping world peace and security. The Anglo-American Dual World Power was pictured, as we will remember, by the "small" horn with eyes and a mouth on the head of the "fourth beast" seen in Daniel's vision of the four beasts.

22-24. How do these not worship the wild beast or its image?

²⁴ The faithful remnant of the 144,000 spiritual Israelites have refused to worship the political "wild beast" by engaging in worship of the State or any of its symbols. They have refused to worship even the most outstanding "head" of the "wild beast," namely, the British-American World Power. And since they refuse to worship the symbolic "wild beast" itself, they consistently refuse to worship its "image" as proposed by the Seventh World Power, the "small" horn with eyes and mouth.—Revelation 13:1-17.

²⁵ Because they refused to worship the political State patriotically, the symbolic "small" horn, the Anglo-American World Power, took action. It harassed this remnant of "the holy ones themselves of the Supreme One," as Daniel 7:25 had foretold. For a test of their devotion to his Messianic kingdom that was set up at the end of the Gentile Times in 1914, the Supreme One gave his "holy ones" into the hands of the symbolic "small" horn "for a time, and times and half a time," or, three years and a half, during World War I. But the sufferings that the "holy ones" endured then and since have failed to force them to compromise.

²⁶ The "holy ones themselves of the Supreme One" know that, even if men put them to death for faithfully living up to the witness that they give to God's Messianic kingdom, they will have a resurrection. Their death is not "the second death" out of which there is no resurrection. (Revelation 2:10, 11; 20:6; 21:8) Spirit-begotten Christians of such full-scale devotion are the

25. For refusing such worship how did they suffer in World War I?
26. What kind of death do such sharers in world rule undergo?

ones whom the Most High God picks out for a share with his Son Jesus Christ in the approaching world government. Could mankind's interests be in safer hands than of those God picks? No!

²⁷ For that potent reason all lovers of righteousness and of incorruptibleness in government can look forward to the thousand-year rule of the King Jesus Christ and his 144,000 associates. Jehovah God as Universal Sovereign has purposed to give to all mankind the best possible government for them. It will be a superhuman world government, fully empowered to undo all the bad effects of the past thousands of years of human misrule and impotence. Before this invincible world government the mighty Seventh World Power and all the other worldly nations within and without the United Nations organization must bow in defeat and vanish during the "great tribulation" now so near. Even Satan the Devil and his demons, the invisible power behind the seven-headed "wild beast" of political rulership, must find all resistance useless. They will be stripped of all their unseen world control and be imprisoned in a sealed abyss for the thousand years of the reign of Christ and his 144,000 joint kings and priests.—Revelation 20:1-3.

²⁸ With eagerness and earnest prayer to the Sovereign Lord Jehovah we look forward to the fulfillment of the assuring words of the angel to Daniel: "And the kingdom and the rulership and the grandeur of the kingdoms under all the heavens were given to the people who are the holy

27. Why will God's government be the best possible for mankind?
28. Why do we eagerly look ahead to such kingdom as very near?

ones of the Supreme One. Their kingdom is an indefinitely lasting kingdom, and all the rulerships will serve and obey even them." (Daniel 7:27) Jehovah's giving of the world rulership to Jesus Christ and all His other "holy ones" must now be very close. For more than nineteen hundred and forty years since Pentecost of 33 C.E., Jehovah has been picking out the 144,000 to be associated with his Holy Son Jesus the Messiah in Kingdom rule over all the earth. By now we must be living in the days of the final remnant of that select body of 144,000 "holy ones." It is also more than sixty years since the Gentile Times ended in October of 1914. Hence the time should be near for the installed heavenly King Jesus Christ to dash the nations to pieces in mankind's greatest time of distress.—Psalm 2:5-9.

²⁹ The "time of the end" is now about to close for the nations! May that never signify the end of us personally along with those worldly nations. (Revelation 19:11-21) May we daily carry out our obligations to the Sovereign Lord Jehovah God so that, if he wills, we may survive into the millennium of Christ's world rule.

---

29. Why do we desire to survive the nations' "time of the end"?

CHAPTER 8

Marked Days During the "Time of the End"

THE "time of the end" has its own end or close. Its grand finale is in a "time of distress" the equal of which the nations have never before experienced nor will again go through. During the said "time of the end" there are marked days. These are time periods that directly affect the "holy ones themselves of the Supreme One," the last remaining ones of the spirit-begotten disciples of Christ who are designated for a share with Jesus Christ in the heavens. These "days" were of such importance as to deserve mention to the aged prophet Daniel of long ago.—Daniel 7:25.

2 In the latter part of chapter eleven of his prophecy, Daniel prophetically points to our present twentieth century and the unrelenting rivalry between the democratic, liberal, capitalistic group of nations and the communistic, totalitarian type of nations. Both blocs of nations have been persecutors of the remaining ones of spirit-begotten "holy ones" of Jehovah God, now known as his Christian witnesses. (Isaiah 43:10-12; 44:8) Daniel closes chapter eleven with a prophetic picture of the final siege by the totalitarian "king of the north" against the remnant of spirit-begotten Witnesses, and then says: "He will have

1. By what time periods is the "time of the end" marked?
2. How will nations persecuting the "holy ones" finally fare?

to come all the way to his end, and there will be no helper for him." His political rival for world domination, the democratic "king of the south," will also be brought to his end with no one to help and save him.—Daniel 11:45.

3 How will such utter destruction of both "the king of the north" and "the king of the south" come about? Jehovah's prophetic angel explained it to Daniel, saying: "And during that time Michael will stand up, the great prince who is standing in behalf of the sons of your people. And there will certainly occur a time of distress such as has not been made to occur since there came to be a nation until that time. And during that time your people will escape, every one who is found written down in the book."—Daniel 12:1.

4 In other Watch Tower Society publications it has been established that Michael, the great heavenly prince who stood in behalf of the sons of Daniel's people back there in the sixth century B.C.E., is the Son of God who became the Lord Jesus Christ. (Daniel 10:13, 21; Jude 9; Revelation 12:7) The sons of Daniel's people back there were the faithful remnant of Israelites who left Babylon and rebuilt Jerusalem and Jehovah's temple there.

5 Today Daniel's people would be, not the fleshly circumcised Israelites who reject the Messiah whose appearing Daniel (9:24, 25) foretold, but the remnant of spiritual Israelites of today, the spirit-begotten Christian witnesses of Jehovah during this twentieth century. In behalf of these spiritual Israelites the glorified Messiah Jesus,

---

3, 4. Who were Michael and the "sons of [Daniel's] people"?
5. In whose behalf does 'Michael the great prince' stand now?

as being once again 'Michael the great prince' in heaven, stands, and he exerts his power and authority in behalf of this spiritual remnant. This action is what precipitates the "time of distress such as has not been made to occur since there came to be a nation until that time."

6 This unprecedented "time of distress" is the "great tribulation" of which the Revelation by means of Jesus speaks and which was illustrated by the destruction of Jerusalem in 70 C.E. as foretold by Jesus Christ. (Revelation 7:14; Matthew 24:21, 22) It is with this "great tribulation" that this now closing "time of the end" reaches its grand finale! During that unparalleled "great tribulation" or "time of distress" the symbolic "king of the north" and "the king of the south" will not escape destruction, but there will be others who will escape. Who? Daniel's people of today, the remnant of spiritual Israelites, "every one who is found written down in the book." (Note Malachi 3:16 and Hebrews 12:23.) Also, Revelation 7:9-17 gives us the assurance that a "great crowd" of worshipers of Daniel's God and believers in the Messiah Jesus will survive along with the spiritual remnant. God keeps a record of his faithful worshipers.

7 What a grand prospect is ahead of us! After that "time of distress" that has no equal in human history there will begin the resurrection of the dead, under God's world government in the hands of his Messiah Jesus, or 'Michael the great prince.' This is the order of events according to what the angel told Daniel, who now goes on to

6. Who will survive the coming "time of distress"?
7, 8. How will dead ones awake to eternal life or to reproach?

tell what the angel said: "And there will be many of those asleep in the ground of dust who will wake up, these to indefinitely lasting life and those to reproaches and to indefinitely lasting abhorrence."—Daniel 12:2.

8 How these former inhabitants of the earth conducted themselves during this life will, of course, affect their initial standing on earth under the Messianic world government. But how they thereafter order their lives under this millennial world government will determine whether they will finally be judged worthy of everlasting life in a Paradise earth or deserving of eternal destruction as objects of reproach and endless abhorrence. Jesus Christ spoke of such possibilities for the resurrected dead, at John 5:28, 29.

9 Glorious then will be the position and privileges of the "holy ones themselves of the Supreme One" to whom the heavenly kingdom and rulership are to be given along with the Messiah Jesus, 'Michael the great prince.' With regard to this the angel went on to say to Daniel: "And the ones having insight will shine like the brightness of the expanse; and those who are bringing the many to righteousness, like the stars to time indefinite, even forever." (Daniel 12:3) Those brought to righteousness under the Messianic world government will be persons who attain to "indefinitely lasting life" in the Paradise earth. But even now, during this "time of the end," the remnant of the "holy ones themselves of the Supreme One" are showing spiritual insight and are therefore busily occupying themselves with

9. What shining ones bring many to righteousness? When?

turning the "great crowd" to righteousness with eternal life on the Paradise earth in view.—Matthew 25:46.

NOW A BOOK UNSEALED

[10] Are we today among those who are turning the many to righteousness or among those who are being turned to righteousness that gives promise of life everlasting? If so, then we can appreciate that we are living in a favored time. Since the end of the Gentile Times in 1914 we have been living in the "time of the end." It is the time for increased spiritual enlightenment, for much of the unexplained prophecies of the Holy Bible, including Daniel's prophecy, to be opened up to our minds and hearts. Ours is the time to which the angel pointed forward when he said to Daniel: "And as for you, O Daniel, make secret the words and seal up the book, until the time of the end. Many will rove about, and the true knowledge will become abundant."—Daniel 12:4.

[11] Today billions of people are much on the move at a fast pace by means of all the modern forms of rapid transportation. Yet these are not the "many" foretold in Daniel 12:4. But after World War I ended in 1918, "many" were the International Bible Students who began to "rove about," how? Mentally, in a deep study of Bible prophecies, including Daniel's prophecy. Long-hidden secrets of God's Word were now due to be unlocked. So these spiritual 'rovers' have had the "true knowledge" of the now unsealed Book of

10. Why is ours the time for enlightenment on Bible prophecy?
11. Who are the 'many rovers' foretold in Daniel 12:4?

God's Word "become abundant" for them. Unselfishly they are spreading this "true knowledge" abroad by word of mouth and by printed page in order that all who want everlasting life under God's world government may act upon this knowledge and thus be turned to righteousness.—Revelation 22:17.

[12] With the prophet Daniel let us listen as one of the angels of his vision asks the question of interest to us also: "How long will it be to the end of the wonderful things?" That is, How long will it be before these portentous things seen by Daniel come to the end of their fulfillment? The answer to the question is given by another angel, who swears with both hands upraised to the truthfulness and reliability of his answer. Daniel says:

[13] "He proceeded to raise his right hand and his left hand to the heavens and to swear by the One who is alive for time indefinite: 'It will be for an appointed time, appointed times and a half. And as soon as there will have been a finishing of the dashing of the power of the holy people to pieces, all these things will come to their finish.'"—Daniel 12:5-7.

[14] Reasonably those three and a half "appointed times" apply to the same period as the three and a half "times" mentioned in Daniel 7:25, during which "times" or "years" the harassed "holy ones themselves of the Supreme One" are given into the hand of the Seventh World Power, symbolized by the "small" horn with eyes and mouth upon

12, 13. How many "times" did the angel swear the prophecy would run?
14. Why were the "holy ones" given into the hand of the "small" horn?

the head of the fourth 'wild beast.' The purpose of the Supreme One's giving his "holy ones" into the hand of the Seventh World Power for that period of time was that there might be a "dashing of the power of the holy people to pieces." Such an action permitted by the Supreme One would demonstrate definitely the hostile attitude of the symbolic "small" horn (yes, too, of the entire "fourth beast") toward the "holy people" who stick to the Universal Sovereignty of the Supreme One.

THE THREE AND A HALF "APPOINTED TIMES"

[15] The end of the three and a half "appointed times" or lunar years was to be marked by the "finishing of the dashing of the power of the holy people to pieces." (Daniel 12:7, *NW; Revised Standard Version; Rotherham; Young*) Of course, this would mean also that the *ability* of the political agent that does the shattering of the power of Jehovah's "holy people" will have come to its end; its ability to do so will no more have its effectiveness or potency. As the Bible translation by Dr. James Moffatt renders it: "It would be three years and half a year, and that when the power of him who shattered the sacred people should be over, then the end of all [things] should arrive." (Also, *An American Translation; The New American Bible*) Thus the political agent that did the shattering during the three and a half years lived on thereafter, but its ability to shatter the power of Jehovah's holy ones again had reached its end. The shattered or dispersed

15. When does the shattering power of the horn prove ineffective?

"holy people" would regather and reorganize and would never again submit to the taking away of their "power."

16 The "finishing of the dashing of the power of the holy people to pieces" evidently occurred on June 21, 1918. On that day the American federal court sentenced the president and the secretary-treasurer of the Watch Tower Bible and Tract Society and five of their headquarters associates to long prison terms, amounting to a total of 140 years. It is true that it was on May 7, 1918, that these officers of the Society and their prominent companions were arrested by federal officers, but they yet had to stand trial and be sentenced, without benefit of bail. So the close of World War I on November 11, 1918, found these seven leading representatives of the International Bible Students, and a close co-worker, in the federal penitentiary at Atlanta, Georgia, U.S.A., to which they had been shipped from Brooklyn, New York, on July 4, 1918. Thus a high court of the Anglo-American Dual World Power did deliver a shattering blow to Jehovah's "holy people" on June 21, 1918.

17 When, therefore, did the three years and a half, which were to be climaxed by that shattering action against dedicated, baptized Christians, begin? How was that beginning marked?

18 Well, June 21, 1918, fell, according to the Biblical lunar calendar, on Tammuz 11, 1918. Three lunar years back from that, or Tammuz 11, 1915, fell on June 23, 1915. Then the half of a lunar year, or six lunar months, back from that would be Tebeth 11, 1914, which coincided with De-

16. When was the "power of the holy people" smashed, and how?
17, 18. So, when did the three and a half lunar years begin?

cember 28, 1914.—See *The Universal Jewish Encyclopedia,* under the heading "Jewish Calendar for 200 Years," pages 634-639.

[19] That date, December 28, 1914, was very appropriate. During the year from early in January the Watch Tower Bible and Tract Society had been showing the famous Photo-Drama of Creation. In that Biblical presentation, which was in four sections of two hours duration for each section, attention was called to Nebuchadnezzar's dream of the world-power "image" and also to the dream of the four political "beasts" that Daniel saw arise out of the sea. Accordingly, notice was served on the nations about the end of the Gentile Times, with catastrophe to follow for all the worldly nations. Further, the battle of Armageddon was warned of, this to be followed by "New Heavens and New Earth." (See pages 50, 51, 92, 94 of the Scenario of the *Photo-Drama of Creation.*) By the month of October, in which month the Gentile Times ended and World War I was raging, the Drama had had showings to large audiences in America, Great Britain, Germany, Switzerland, Denmark, Sweden, Finland, Australia and New Zealand.—*The Watch Tower,* issue of December 15, 1914, pages 371, 372.

[20] In the issue of January 1, 1915, in presenting "View from the Watch Tower," the *Watch Tower* magazine opened up, saying: "When our worthy President [Thomas Woodrow Wilson] and also his Holiness the Pope requested Christian people to pray God for the cessation of the European

19. The Photo-Drama of Creation served what notice on the nations?
20. What did the next *Watch Tower* issue after December 28, 1914, say about prayers requested for World War I to end?

war, we declared that the prayer was not in harmony with the Divine arrangement and would not be answered. We pointed out that according to the Scriptures the 2520 years of Gentile dominion ended in September, 1914; and that the war is the one predicted in the Scriptures as associated with the Great Day of Almighty God—'the Day of Vengeance of our God.' We pointed out the Word of the Lord through the Prophet Joel respecting the gathering of all nations to the Valley of Jehoshaphat—the valley of death. —Joel 3:1-12." In agreement with this line of thought, the first study article of that same magazine issue was entitled "The First Armageddon Battle."—Page 7.

[21] Persecution was then expected for the congregations of the International Bible Students, for, under the heading "1915—Our Year Text—1915," the same issue of *The Watch Tower* opened up by saying: "We have chosen as a text for the year the Master's words uttered just before His crucifixion to two of His dear disciples, who had asked to sit with Him in His Throne. We have selected the Master's reply as the text for this year: 'Are ye able to drink of My cup?'—Matthew 20:20-23." (Page 11) By then ten nations and empires were in the war and more were to get in during 1915 and thereafter until finally twenty-eight nations and empires became involved in World War I. So Jehovah's "holy people," then known as International Bible Students, could not escape persecutions and sufferings such as are included in the 'drinking of the cup' of their Master, Jesus Christ.

---

21. How did the Year Text for 1915 show sufferings were expected?

²² Ever since the year 1876 those who became associated with the Watch Tower Bible and Tract Society and the International Bible Students Association had been publicly declaring that the Gentile Times would terminate in early autumn of 1914. Accordingly, they warned the whole world of the destruction of those Gentile nations to make way for God's millennial kingdom in the hands of his glorified Son Jesus Christ. As these dedicated, baptized and spirit-anointed Christians had proclaimed the approaching destruction of all the worldly nations, including the British Empire and the United States of North America, these nations set out to destroy these proclaimers of God's kingdom by Christ. They used the situation created by World War I to do so.—Note Revelation 11:3-10; 13:1, 2, 5, 7.

²³ On July 17, 1917, the Watch Tower Bible and Tract Society released the book entitled "The Finished Mystery." This book dealt with Revelation and the prophecy of Ezekiel and, unavoidably, it emphasized the destruction of religious Babylon the Great and her political, military, judicial and commercial friends. (James 4:4) This provided further basis for the political authorities, egged on by the clergy of Babylon the Great, to 'dash to pieces the power of Jehovah's holy people.' This they accomplished by the end of the foretold three and a half years on June 21, 1918. Thus this period began on December 28, 1914, in the first northern winter of World War I. By then the International Bible Students, who were conscientious objectors to carnal warfare, felt the

22. Since 1876 what had they warned the nations about 1914?
23. In 1917 what book provided further basis for persecution?

mounting pressure upon them to compromise in the embattled British Empire, the German Empire, the Austro-Hungarian Empire, the French Empire, Belgium, and the five other nations then engaged in the spreading world conflict. Their Bible text chosen for 1915 indicated that fact. So the period of three and a half "times" is well marked!

24 The prophet Daniel could not, of course, envision how all the portentous things that had been disclosed to him would work out in modern history. He himself said: "Now as for me, I heard, but I could not understand; so that I said: 'O my lord, what will be the final part of these things?' And he went on to say: 'Go, Daniel, because the words are made secret and sealed up until the time of the end. Many will cleanse themselves and whiten themselves and will be refined. And the wicked ones will certainly act wickedly, and no wicked ones at all will understand; but the ones having insight will understand.' "—Daniel 12:8-10.

25 Daniel "could not understand" what he heard, in his day. But we, in this day, in this "time of the end" since 1914, can understand. But not if we "act wickedly." How, then, are we acting? Wickedly, or with spiritual insight? It results differently!

26 Let us think seriously about what the angel said to Daniel about the impending "time of distress," namely, that Daniel's "people will escape, every one who is found written down in the book." (Daniel 12:1) Do we desire to be

---

24. Did Daniel understand the vision? What reason was given?
25, 26. Therefore, in what class mentioned do we want to be found?

associated with Daniel's "people"? Then it is our business to avoid being found among those acting wickedly in this time of the end. We want our names to be "found written down in the book" of God. To this end we need to exercise "insight" by consulting God's Word, learning its instructive message for our crucial day and then acting in accord with God's will. Let the "true knowledge" abound for us!

THE 1,290 DAYS AND THE 1,335 DAYS

[27] Regarding the prophetic information given to Daniel, the angel said: "The words are made secret and sealed up until the time of the end." (Daniel 12:9) The fact that the once secret and sealed "words" are now unsealed and brought out of secrecy adds to the abundance of proof that, since the end of the Gentile Times in 1914, we have been in the exciting "time of the end." We see how the "appointed time, appointed times and a half" of Daniel 12:7 have fitted into this "time of the end." Although those three and a half years are now so far in the past, yet they marked a turning point in the course of the remnant of Daniel's modern-day "people," so that this has affected the Christian witnesses of Jehovah who are alive today. But there are other time periods that are assigned by Jehovah to this interesting "time of the end," and Daniel 12:11, 12 now brings these to our attention:

[28] "And from the time that the constant feature has been removed and there has been a placing of the disgusting thing that is causing desolation,

---

27-29. What other periods were foretold for the "time of the end"?

there will be one thousand two hundred and ninety days.

29 "Happy is the one who is keeping in expectation and who arrives at the one thousand three hundred and thirty-five days!"

30 Here, for our guidance in understanding matters, we must bear in mind that religious Babylon the Great does *not* place or establish "the disgusting thing that is causing desolation." The political elements of this system of things do this. For the "one thousand two hundred and ninety days" to start, both requirements must be met, namely, the "constant feature" must be removed *and* the "disgusting thing that is causing desolation" must be put in place. The removing of the "constant feature" took place during the "appointed time, appointed times and a half" that ran their course during World War I, from December 28, 1914, to sundown of June 21, 1918. The "constant feature" had to do with Jehovah's "holy people," whose spiritual "power" was dashed to pieces back there.

31 In 537 B.C.E. the prophet Daniel's people were released from ancient Babylon by the conqueror, Cyrus the Persian, and they returned to the land of Judah to reestablish Jehovah's worship at Jerusalem. There, at the end of the seventy years of desolation of their homeland, they proceeded to "build the altar of the God of Israel, to offer up burnt sacrifices upon it, according to what is written in the law of Moses the man of the true God." (Ezra 3:1, 2) From then on the "constant feature" of each day was offered by the

30. Who sets up the "disgusting thing" that causes desolation?
31. What was the "constant feature" offered by Daniel's people?

priests, with the exception of a temporary interruption by the Syrians during the days of the Levite Maccabees in the second century B.C.E. (Exodus 29:28, 29) What, though, was the "constant feature" of each day that the spiritual Israelites were offering up to God at the beginning of the "time of the end" in 1914?

[32] It did not consist of animal sacrifices offered upon an altar at Jerusalem in the Middle East. Such sacrifices ceased to be offered there in the year 70 C.E. at the destruction of Jerusalem and its gorgeous temple by the Roman legions. Years before that, the Christian apostle Peter wrote, saying that the anointed spiritual Israelites "are being built up a spiritual house for the purpose of a holy priesthood, to offer up spiritual sacrifices acceptable to God through Jesus Christ." (1 Peter 2:5, 9) These "spiritual sacrifices" include "a sacrifice of praise, that is, the fruit of lips which make public declaration to his name." (Hebrews 13:15) After the Gentile Times ended in 1914 and God's Messianic kingdom was born in the heavens, the "sacrifice of praise" as part of the "constant feature" that was offered by the spiritual Israelites consisted particularly of bearing witness to the established heavenly kingdom in the hands of Jesus Christ.—Matthew 24:3, 14.

[33] By harassing the anointed Kingdom witnesses and finally by dashing to pieces their spiritual "power" for proclaiming God's kingdom that must supersede all man-made governments on earth, the warring nations suppressed the Kingdom witnesses and thus removed the "constant feature."

---

32. Of what did the "constant feature" since 1914 C.E. consist?
33. When was removal of the "constant feature" accomplished?

This was accomplished by June 21, 1918. For eight months and four days thereafter the sentenced officers of the Watch Tower Bible and Tract Society and their colaborers lingered in federal imprisonment, awaiting their being released on bail for a new trial and exoneration from all the false charges. Their unjust imprisonment for so long acted as a great deterrent to the offering of the "constant feature" by the Kingdom witnesses. But what about the "disgusting thing" that desolates?

[34] The "disgusting thing that is causing desolation" is the international organization for world peace and security. This was first designed by the peace conference that assembled in Versailles, France, on January 18, 1919. The victorious war allies drew up the peace treaty that was submitted to the German delegates on May 7, 1919. On June 28, 1919, the German and the Allied delegates signed this peace treaty at Versailles. The international organization for world peace and security, then known as the League of Nations, was part and parcel of that peace treaty, and when the governments involved ratified the signed peace treaty, the League of Nations went into force.

[35] Prior to that, when the peace conference that paved the way for the League of Nations met on January 18, 1919, the clergy of the Church of England and the Federal Council of the Churches of Christ in America had come out in favor of the proposed League and pressed for the creation

34. How was the "disgusting thing" brought into existence?
35. How did the clergy of Christendom back up the League of Nations?

of it. The clergy hailed it as "the political expression of the Kingdom of God on earth."

[36] If, now, we measure 1,290 days from that marked date, January 18, 1919, when the eight representatives of the Watch Tower Bible and Tract Society were still under restraint in the Atlanta federal penitentiary, where do we end up? According to the Bible, those 1,290 days are the equivalent of three lunar years and seven lunar months. According to the lunar calendar, January 18, 1919, fell on Shebat 17, 1919. Three lunar years from then would lead up to Shebat 17, 1922, or February 15, 1922. Seven lunar months counted from that would end with Elul 16, 1922, or at sundown, September 9, 1922. So did the 1,290 days or three lunar years and seven months end at a significant time? The historical facts answer Yes!

[37] The following day, September 10, 1922, a Sunday, proved to be the sixth day of a nine-day international convention of the International Bible Students Association at Cedar Point, Ohio, U.S.A. It was entitled on the program as "Activity Day." The feature of the day was the public address to an audience of 18,000, by the president of the Watch Tower Bible and Tract Society. At the close of his oral argument, the speaker submitted to his audience a resolution called "A Proclamation," which set forth a challenge to all the world rulers. This Proclamation was meant, not for just those conventioners, but for all the world, and subsequent to the Cedar Point convention it was published in tract form and distributed by the tens of millions of copies in many languages.

36. So, when did the 1,290 days begin and end?
37. How was the following day, September 10, 1922, marked?

[38] The preceding day, Saturday, September 9, was entitled "Consecration Day" and was marked by the mass baptism of 361 men and women in symbol of their dedication to God through Christ. However, Friday, September 8, was entitled "The Day," which featured the address of the Society's president on the theme found in Matthew 4:17: "The Kingdom of Heaven Is at Hand." (AV) Leading up to the climax of his address, the speaker said:

> "Why, then, deliver the message to those who do not understand? Will any one hear? The Prophet of the Lord answers: 'Bring forth the blind people that have eyes, and the deaf that have ears. Let all the nations be gathered together, and let the people be assembled: who among them can declare this, and shew us former things? let them bring forth their witnesses, that they may be justified: or let them hear, and say, It is truth. Ye are my witnesses, saith the Lord, and my servant whom I have chosen: that ye may know and believe me, and understand that I am he: before me there was no God formed, neither shall there be after me. I, even I, am the Lord; and beside me there is no saviour. I have declared, and have saved, and I have shewed, when there was no strange god among you: therefore ye are my witnesses, saith the Lord, that I am God.'—Isaiah 43:8-12.

> "Thus we see that those of the temple class are clearly designated as the Lord's witnesses at this time, to bring a message of consolation to the people, that the kingdom of heaven is here, . . . "

So, with all due fitness, the Society's president could close his rousing speech with this exhortation: "Advertise, advertise, advertise, the King and his kingdom."

---

38. What featured September 9, 1922, itself, and September 8?

39 Immediate opportunity to advertise was offered on the day after the public talk and the challenging resolution adopted by all the conventioners. That Monday, September 11, 1922, was entitled "Service Day," and the conventioners sallied forth into the field service, more keenly aware than ever that they were advance publicity agents of God's glorious kingdom.

40 Later on, it was discerned that the public message and the resolution adopted in connection with that public message was the start of the fulfillment of what was foretold in Revelation, chapters eight through sixteen. What was that? The sounding of the seven trumpets and the pouring out of the seven last plagues of Jehovah's wrath upon this doomed system of things.

41 Calculating the 1,290 days of Daniel 12:11 in this here-given way, do we find that they terminated at a very significant time? We have every reason to believe so. There can be little question that the 1,290 days thus calculated mark an epoch for Jehovah's "holy people" in this time of the end. The supreme issue before the whole universe was then coming to the fore, namely, Jehovah's Universal Sovereignty.

HAPPINESS AFTER 1,335 DAYS

42 What, now, about the one thousand three hundred and thirty-five days as marked out in Daniel 12:12? The angel said nothing about when these days were to begin; he merely indicated that they would end with the expectant ones en-

39. How was Monday, September 11, 1922, marked?
40. What expression of God's wrath was thus started publicly?
41. What supreme issue was thus coming to the fore universally?
42. The close of the 1,335 days was to be marked with what?

tering into a happiness of noteworthy degree: "Happy is the one who is keeping in expectation and who arrives at the one thousand three hundred and thirty-five days!" Evidently these 1,335 days are an extension of time beyond the 1,290 days just mentioned, which had ended in the midst of the I.B.S.A. convention at Cedar Point, Ohio, in 1922. Such an extension of time—for 1,335 days more—called for further endurance on the part of the remnant of Jehovah's "holy people" that had survived World War I. They had little idea then of the happiness that would be bestowed upon them for enduring and arriving at the end of those 1,335 days. So—when did those days begin and end?

[43] The second Cedar Point convention ended on September 13, 1922. If, now, we count from the next day, September 14, or, Elul 21, 1922, Bible calendar time, when would the 1,335 days end? As the 1,290 days amounted to three lunar years and seven months, so the 1,335 days would amount to three lunar years, eight months and fifteen days. Counting now *from* Elul 21 (or, September 14), 1922, we find that three lunar years from that date would end on Elul 20 (or, September 9), 1925. To this we add eight lunar months and fifteen days and arrive at the date Sivan 6 (or, May 19), 1926. That day was the 1,893rd anniversary of the happy day of Pentecost of 33 C.E., when the holy spirit was poured out upon Jesus' disciples at Jerusalem.

[44] Just prior to this, on May 13-16, 1926, a general assembly had taken place in Magdeburg,

43. By the Bible calendar, when did the 1,335 days end?
44. What closely preceded and what closely followed that day?

Germany, at which the president of the Watch Tower Society had addressed a public audience of 25,000 on the subject "Comfort for the People." Now, on May 19, preparations moved ahead for the holding of the outstanding international convention of 1926, that at Alexandra Palace, London, England, May 25-31. Many happy delegates came from distant lands.

[45] This London assembly made a tremendous contribution to the happiness of the prophet Daniel's people, the remnant of spiritual Israelites. At that time, not too many people were really happy about the taking over of Italy by the Fascists. Fears were excited by the progress of the Nazi (National Socialist German Workers' Party) movement in Germany. But the six-year-old League of Nations was going strong and was about to admit postwar Germany to its membership—on September 8, 1926. In spite of this the International Bible Students Association (I.B.S.A.) continued to expose the League as a man-made political substitute for God's kingdom that had come to power in the heavens since the end of the Gentile Times in 1914. These Christian Bible Students had responded to the question, "Who will honor Jehovah?" that the *Watch Tower* issue of January 1, 1926, had raised before its readers, and had chosen to honor Jehovah and his kingdom.

[46] On Friday, May 28, J. F. Rutherford as president of the Watch Tower Bible and Tract Society submitted to the London conventioners the resolution entitled "A Testimony to the Rulers of

---

45. By then whom had the Christian Bible Students chosen to honor?
46. What marked Friday, May 28, of the 1926 London convention?

the World." This was the fifth in a series of resolutions adopted at annual conventions of the I.B.S.A. This London resolution together with its supporting message proved to be the start of the pouring out of the fifth "plague" as foretold in Revelation 16:10, 11. Quite significantly that fifth plague began to be poured out at London, England, the capital of the British Empire, which was the British member of the Seventh World Power of Bible prophecy, the Anglo-American Dual World Power, the most mighty of all the world powers of history. The corporate offices of the I.B.S.A. were located in London.

[47] On Saturday, May 29, the whole day was devoted to the field service. Said the printed convention program: "This day is set aside for field service. Every consecrated one attending the convention is invited to share in advertising the King and the Kingdom. Get to the Alexandra Palace as early as possible, and report for service at the Service Department. A motor-car service is being arranged for places further afield."

[48] Those of us still alive who attended that London convention will remember how we boarded city buses in groups and were taken to our locations throughout the city to offer a new booklet on the sidewalks and at the Underground entrances. In this way 120,000 copies of the booklet *The Standard for the People* were placed in the hands of passersby. Reporting on this then unusual way of advertising the King and the Kingdom, *The Watch Tower*, under date of July 15, 1926, said: "Nothing like this has ever been known on Service Day at a convention. The friends

---

47, 48. What unusual activity marked Saturday, May 29, 1926?

were bubbling over with enthusiasm. They felt that they had done their best to obey the command of Jehovah: 'Ye are my witnesses that I am God.' "

⁴⁹ Sunday, May 30, crowned the happiness and blessing of this history-making convention, with about 4,000 present. At 2:00 p.m., there was a baptismal service at the Alexandra Palace, after which 184 were immersed in water as dedicated witnesses of the Most High God. That night, the conventioners moved over to Britain's then largest auditorium, the Royal Albert Hall, for the public lecture by the I.B.S.A. president, J. F. Rutherford, on the subject "Why World Powers Are Tottering —The Remedy." The Hall was packed to overflowing, with more than 10,000 present. After the reading of the Resolution "A Testimony to the Rulers of the World," President Rutherford proceeded with his talk. He led up to the Eighth World Power as foretold in Bible prophecy, then the League of Nations, and pointed forward to the failure of such an international organization for world peace and security. Human rule of mankind would end up in the world's greatest catastrophe, and then would come The Remedy, God's kingdom by Christ, with peace, prosperity, health, life and happiness for all humankind. In conclusion, the speaker said:

⁵⁰ "Let the kings and rulers of the earth now give their allegiance and devotion to the Lord. Let them acknowledge Jehovah as God, and Christ Jesus as his anointed King; and thus doing they will render a real service to the people and put themselves in line for the eternal blessings of

49. What events marked Sunday, May 30, 1926, at London?
50. In conclusion, what did the public speaker say in appeal?

Jehovah." The following day one of London's newspapers came out with a full report of this public lecture spreading across an entire page, so that many more thousands read this challenging Kingdom message than heard it at Royal Albert Hall. So the foretold fifth "plague" was indeed being poured out!

[51] The final day of the convention, Monday, May 31, 1926, the conventioners went out afield to place in the hands of the Jewish population of London a paperbound book especially written for them. That night the conventioners again moved over to the Royal Albert Hall to attend what proved to be a final large-scale public appeal to the Jews to turn to Jehovah's Messiah, his now reigning Son Jesus Christ. There thousands of Jews responded to the public advertising and heard the Society's president give them a stirring message that should have been for their comfort. Their only hope was in Jehovah's Messiah. The choice was now up to circumcised natural Israelites!

[52] Among the notable features of this most happy convention of Jehovah's remnant of *spiritual* Israelites was the public release on Friday, May 28, of the Society's new publication entitled "Deliverance." For the Biblical enlightenment this book gave, it was a thriller for Jehovah's people. As no previous publication had done, it made God's organization prominent, as symbolized by the woman in Revelation, chapter twelve, and drew a sharp contrast between God's organization and Satan's organization. This book was the first of a series of books that replaced the seven volumes

---

51. How was the final convention day, May 31, marked?
52. What thrilling book was released Friday, May 28, 1926?

of *Studies in the Scriptures* (of 1886-1917), which had served as the standard of Bible instruction till then. The following year there appeared the book *Creation* (1927), thereafter *Reconciliation* (1928), *Government* (1928), *Life* (1929), *Light* (in two volumes, 1930), *Vindication* (in three volumes, 1931, 1932), *Preservation* (1932), *Preparation* (1933), *Jehovah* (1934), and so forth, down till this year.

[53] Furthermore, at the 1926 convention held in the capital of the British Empire, the Watch Tower Society's president assigned experienced men to posts of service in foreign fields, including two who were to open up a new branch in Bombay, India, then a British colony. (See the *Year Book I.B.S.A.*, copyrighted in 1926, page 90.) Also, he promoted arrangements for publishing the Society's annual report in book form. So, in due time, in order to put on record the Kingdom activities of Jehovah's people for the significant year of 1926, there appeared the "Year Book of the International Bible Students Association with Daily Texts and Comments." (320 pages) The "Daily Heavenly Manna and Birthday Records," which had been used in daily Christian worship since its publication in 1907, now went out of use, as new daily texts and comments appeared in each succeeding *Year Book* published by the Watch Tower Bible and Tract Society down to date.

[54] During the past half century not a *Year Book* has failed to appear with each passing year, setting forth in great detail the worldwide ac-

---

53, 54. (a) What expansion was arranged for at the 1926 London convention? (b) Also, what annual publication was promoted?

tivities of Jehovah's Christian witnesses in preaching this good news of the Kingdom.—Matthew 24:14.

⁵⁵ Another important thing that added to the happy outlook of Jehovah's people at the time of the international convention in London was this: Plans were under consideration for the Watch Tower Bible and Tract Society to build an eight-story factory of its own at Brooklyn, New York, to meet the requirements of the expanding witness work world wide. On July 23, 1926, the real estate for this was finally purchased. In spite of the following winter, the construction of this Society-owned factory progressed.

⁵⁶ Great was the joy of members of the Brooklyn headquarters staff when they moved into this specially designed, spacious factory and office building in February of 1927. So on the publisher's page of the *Watch Tower* magazine issue of February 1, 1927, and of *The Golden Age* issue of February 9, 1927, there appeared the Publisher's address: 117 Adams Street, Brooklyn, New York. This building had to be added to later, and it became the nucleus of a growth of thirty-two printing plants related to the Watch Tower Bible and Tract Society around the globe. Output of Bible study literature by this globe-encircling printing chain till now has been enormous. Thereby a spiritual Paradise has spread!

⁵⁷ Truly the year 1926 deserved to be marked as the happy climax of the close of the 1,335 days. Those of Daniel's "people" who kept in expectation and reached the end of the 1,335 days were

55. What building program added to the remnant's happiness?
56. Of what did that factory prove to be the nucleus?
57. Into a happiness of what duration did the remnant enter?

launched off into a happiness that has not diminished, but that, despite mounting persecution and World War II (1939-1945) and subsequent world troubles, has persisted and increased. Particularly from that marked year of 1926 the dedicated, baptized worshipers of the God and Father of our Lord Jesus Christ have entered into the Paradisaic happiness expressed by the inspired psalmist, when he said: "Happy is the nation whose God is Jehovah, the people whom he has chosen as his inheritance."—Psalms 33:12; 144:15b.

⁵⁸ The prophet Daniel was not privileged to see and enter into this happiness of the Christian witnesses of his God, Jehovah. He was told not to expect to do so, for God's angel said to him: "And as for you yourself, go toward the end; and you will rest, but you will stand up for your lot at the end of the days." (Daniel 12:13) For more than 2,500 years now Daniel has rested in the grave, in the sleep of death. In due time he will stand up in the resurrection to receive his lot under the Messianic kingdom of Jehovah God, about which he was inspired to prophesy so marvelously. (Hebrews 11:33-40) Moreover, God's due time draws near when, not only Daniel, but also Abraham, Isaac, Jacob, Moses and all the other faithful prophets of old will stand up for their "lot," waking up from the sleep of death "to indefinitely lasting life" and to the opportunity of serving as "princes in all the earth" under our incoming world government.—Psalm 45:16; Daniel 12:2.

58. After all those "days," into what lot will Daniel enter?

CHAPTER 9

The "Sign" of Imminence of the World Government

HOW HAPPY we can be that rule of all the earth by political governments of imperfect men is nearing its end! At the same time the perfect world government promised by God is imminent. The proof of this is available today. Since the year 1914 we have discerned the unfolding, unerring "sign" of this. Nineteen centuries ago a prophet greater than Daniel described that "sign" in detail. We can now read its meaning if we will. The Describer of this timely "sign" made reference to things foretold in Daniel, chapter twelve. For instance, along in his great prophecy he said to his twelve apostles on the Mount of Olives:

² "And this good news of the kingdom will be preached in all the inhabited earth for a witness to all the nations; and then the end will come. Therefore, when you catch sight of the disgusting thing that causes desolation, as spoken of through Daniel the prophet, standing in a holy place, (let the reader use discernment,) then let those in Judea begin fleeing to the mountains. Let the man on the housetop not come down to take the goods out of his house; and let the man in the

---

1, 2. (a) Proof of imminence of God's world government is furnished in what? (b) What needs to be done before the "great tribulation"?

field not return to the house to pick up his outer garment. Woe to the pregnant women and those suckling a baby in those days! Keep praying that your flight may not occur in wintertime, nor on the sabbath day; for then there will be great tribulation such as has not occurred since the world's beginning until now, no, nor will occur again. In fact, unless those days were cut short, no flesh would be saved; but on account of the chosen ones those days will be cut short."—Matthew 24:14-22; Mark 13:14-20.

³ Back in the days of the apostles of Jesus Christ the "holy place" was the city of Jerusalem with its gorgeous temple for the worship of Jehovah as God. Judea was a Roman province, of which Jerusalem was the religious capital. The "disgusting thing that is causing desolation," as referred to at Daniel 12:11, was the military legions of the Roman Empire, the Sixth World Power of Bible prophecy. By a violent military attack the "disgusting thing" of that day was "standing" for a time in the "holy place" in the autumn of the year 66 C.E. That was a warning signal to the Christianized Jews still residing in Jerusalem. So, after the "disgusting thing" withdrew temporarily from Jerusalem, the now duly warned Christians obediently fled from the doomed "holy place." Many of these fugitives fled to the "mountains" in the Roman province of Perea on the other side of the Jordan River.

⁴ It was well that those Christianized Jews did so, for, four years later, the "disgusting thing"

---

3. When did Christianized Jews flee from the "holy place"? Why?
4. What things came as foretold on that Jewish generation?

returned. It desolated all the province of Judea and capped the desolation by destroying both Jerusalem and its holy temple in a "great tribulation" that shocked Jews inside and outside the Roman Empire. The Christianized Jews in safe places of refuge outside Judea survived Jerusalem's destruction in 70 C.E. Some Jewish "flesh" that had remained inside the rebellious city also survived, but only to be carried off captive by the Romans. So that generation of unchristianized Jews did not act on the "sign" that Jesus Christ had foretold. For that generation he had foretold wars, famines, pestilences, earthquakes, persecution of Christians, lawlessness, Kingdom preaching world wide, and the standing of the "disgusting thing" in the "holy place." All these things had come upon that generation of Jews as a "sign" to them of the fast-approaching destruction of the Jewish system of things.—Matthew 24:3-22; Luke 21:10-23.

THE CLIMAX OF THE MODERN-DAY "SIGN" IMMINENT

[5] However, was Jerusalem's destruction in 70 C.E. followed by God's world government in the hands of Jesus Christ, the worthy Descendant of King David? No! The Roman Empire continued on as the Sixth World Power and kept increasing to attain its greatest dominion in the reign of Emperor Trajan. So the Gentile Times of 2,520 years of duration moved on toward their termination in 1914 C.E. History worked just as Jesus had foretold: "Jerusalem will be trampled on by

---

5. Why did God's world government not follow Jerusalem's ruin?

the [Gentile] nations, until the appointed times of the nations are fulfilled." (Luke 21:24) The Seventh Gentile World Power was yet to arise in the form of the Anglo-American Dual World Power, starting in 1763 C.E. It still functions, and the American member of that Dual World Power celebrated its two hundredth anniversary, its bicentennial, on July 4, 1976. That celebration was nearly sixty-two years after the Gentile Times ended in the year 1914.

6 Not only the United States of America and the British Commonwealth of Nations but all the other Gentile nations refuse to recognize God's Messianic kingdom, the birth of which was repeatedly called to their attention.—Revelation 12:1-5.

7 The "presence" or *parousia* of the glorified Messiah Jesus in Kingdom authority is an accomplished fact since 1914! How much longer will Jehovah's enthroned, crowned Messianic King put up with the combined resistance of earthly political governments now that their lease of world domination without God's interference has expired? Not much longer, if we are to judge by the details of the foretold "sign of [Christ's] presence [*parousia*] and of the conclusion of the system of things."—Matthew 24:3.

8 Jesus Christ had our generation in mind as well as the Jewish generation of his day, when he said: "Truly I say to you that this generation will by no means pass away until all these things

6. What nations refuse to recognize God's newborn kingdom?
7. How much longer will Christ put up with resistant nations?
8. To whom does the word "generation" in Matthew 24:34 apply?

occur. Heaven and earth will pass away, but my words will by no means pass away."—Matthew 24:34, 35.

⁹ Well, then, what are we of "this generation" yet waiting for? We have seen, heard, and experienced the international wars, famines, pestilences, earthquakes, worldwide persecution of Jehovah's Christian witnesses, increase of lawlessness, decrease of love of God by the majority, and the preaching of "this good news of the kingdom" by the Christian witnesses of Jehovah since 1914 C.E. We have gone through these things in fuller measure than did the Jewish "generation" of nineteen hundred years ago. We have witnessed the removal of the "constant feature" of Jehovah's worship during World War I by the persecutions heaped upon Jehovah's worshipers by the warring nations. We have also observed the "placing of the disgusting thing that is causing desolation" in the 'setting up' of a man-made substitute for God's Messianic kingdom, namely, the League of Nations, in 1919, and its successor, the United Nations, in 1945. (Matthew 24:4-15; Daniel 12:11) So what is "this generation" shortly to expect?

"KNOW THAT HE IS NEAR AT THE DOORS"

¹⁰ With a swift skipping of intervening centuries of our Common Era, Jesus Christ passed from the "great tribulation" that resulted in Jerusalem's destruction in 70 C.E. down to our critical period, "the time of the end." (Daniel 12:4) He said:

---

9. What has "this generation" already seen fulfilled since 1914?
10-12. For "this generation" of today, what does Matthew 24: 23-31 say?

[11] "Then if anyone says to you, 'Look! Here is the Christ,' or, 'There!' do not believe it. For false Christs and false prophets will arise and will give great signs and wonders so as to mislead, if possible, even the chosen ones. Look! I have forewarned you. Therefore, if people say to you, 'Look! He is in the wilderness,' do not go out; 'Look! He is in the inner chambers,' do not believe it. For just as the lightning comes out of eastern parts and shines over to western parts, so the presence [*parousia*] of the Son of man will be. Wherever the carcass is, there the eagles will be gathered together.

[12] "Immediately after the tribulation of those days the sun will be darkened, and the moon will not give its light, and the stars will fall from heaven, and the powers of the heavens will be shaken. And then the sign of the Son of man will appear in heaven, and then all the tribes of the earth will beat themselves in lamentation, and they will see the Son of man coming on the clouds of heaven with power and great glory. And he will send forth his angels with a great trumpet sound, and they will gather his chosen ones together from the four winds, from one extremity of the heavens to their other extremity."—Matthew 24:23-31; Mark 13:21-27.

[13] Like a "great trumpet sound" the message foretold in Matthew 24:14, "this good news of the kingdom," has been increasingly sounded forth world wide since the year 1919 by the present-day remnant of "his chosen ones." The more of these

---

13. How do we know that the remnant of "chosen ones" are with us?

"chosen ones" that have been gathered from the four cardinal points ("the four winds"), the louder or more widespread has been the sound of the "good news" trumpet. For this reason we know that the "chosen ones" who are in line for a place in the heavenly kingdom are with us in this "time of the end." We have not visibly seen any spirit angels gathering them together, but we *do* see the effect of such angelic activities according to the will of the glorified Son of man. By their preaching work publicly and from house to house, the remnant of gathered "chosen ones" have made themselves seen and heard.

[14] No, they have not been gathered under angelic guidance into any one place in any one land. Rather, they have been gathered into a worldwide unity of thought and activity according to the unfolding Holy Scriptures, and they regularly meet together in their congregations, in homes or in Kingdom Halls. Even when banned by hostile worldly governments, they persist in gathering together, "underground," so to speak, to build one another up in Christian faith and to organize their preaching efforts. At their annual celebration of the Lord's Supper, the commemoration of Christ's death on Nisan 14 (Bible calendar), they partake of the emblematic bread and wine. On April 14 (Nisan 14), of the year 1976, 10,187 of such "chosen ones" thus celebrated and partook of the emblems.

[15] These faithful "chosen ones" are waiting for the "sign of the Son of man" in the heavens as

14. Into what have the angels gathered the "chosen ones"?
15. The gathered remnant now look for what "sign" to appear?

he comes in the role of God's Executioner to destroy all the nations who continue in opposition to his Messianic kingdom over all the earth. No wonder that, when he makes his presence felt by his destructive operations, it will be as if they actually *saw* him "coming on the clouds of heaven with power and great glory." All good reason for them to "beat themselves in lamentation."—Matthew 24:30; Revelation 1:7.

THE POINT TO BE LEARNED NOW

[16] We are, or at least we all should be, interested in knowing whether the grand climax of developments will come in our time. How can we know the possibility of this and be guided accordingly? For the guidance of us living today, Jesus as the Prophet concerning the "conclusion of the system of things" went on to say to his twelve apostles: "Now learn from the fig tree as an illustration this point: Just as soon as its young branch grows tender and it puts forth leaves, you know that summer is near. Likewise also you, when you see all these things, know that he is near at the doors. Truly I say to you that this generation will by no means pass away until all these things occur. Heaven and earth will pass away, but my words will by no means pass away."—Matthew 24:32-35; compare Luke 21:27-33.

[17] Those of the "chosen ones" alive today who witnessed the outbreak of World War I in 1914 can recall how we all rejoiced because we saw "these things start to occur." We knew that the

16. What illustrates how we can know he is near at the doors?
17. We who saw these things start, do what and know what?

newly enthroned Christ was "near at the doors" for his executional work against this wicked "system of things." We exulted because "the kingdom of God is near" for taking over full world control and functioning as a world government. We have not grown tired of being reminded over and over again during these past sixty years and more that the Messianic kingdom of God is "near at the doors." This reminding of us has not grown stale and lost its potency and soul-stirring force toward us. We know that we are of the "generation" that saw the start of these things in 1914 at the close of the Gentile Times, and we believe Jesus' assurance that this same "generation" of ours will see the finish of these significant things, all this culminating in the total take-over by the triumphant Kingdom of all human affairs.

[18] A global catastrophe affecting far more people and institutions than the deluge of Noah's day affected is about to break upon this "world of ungodly people." (2 Peter 2:5) This needs to be—it deserves to be—drummed into the ears of the "chosen ones" and of all others who are interested in a perfect, righteous world government. This is not a case of frightening people with a false scare like that of the God-defaming doctrine of "eternal torment in a hell of literal fire and brimstone" in order to force their conversion and their attendance at some church. Not merely the life, but the *eternal* life, of the imperiled people is at stake, and, as God's appointed 'watchmen,' we are under obligation to warn honest-hearted,

---

18. Is our warning people just a scaring of them to do right?

righteously disposed persons. (Ezekiel 3:17-21; 33:6-20) We do not wish to come short of our responsibilities toward God. We are not *frightening ourselves* into doing our duty when we take this matter seriously. Our aim is to display love toward God and toward our fellow humans, especially our Christian brothers.

[19] Jesus Christ himself did not want to preach and prophesy to no purpose. He did not want his warning to be in vain for his disciples, when he said to them: "Concerning that day and hour nobody knows, neither the angels of the heavens nor the Son, but only the Father. For just as the days of Noah were, so the presence [*parousia*] of the Son of man will be. For as they were in those days before the flood, eating and drinking, men marrying and women being given in marriage, until the day [!] that Noah entered into the ark; and they took no note until the flood came and swept them all away, so the presence of the Son of man will be. Then two men will be in the field: one will be taken along and the other be abandoned; two women will be grinding at the hand mill: one will be taken along and the other be abandoned. Keep on the watch, therefore, because you do not know on what day your Lord is coming.

[20] "But know one thing, that if the householder had known in what watch the thief was coming, he would have kept awake and not allowed his house to be broken into. On this account you too prove yourselves ready, because at an hour that

19, 20. Did Jesus want his warning to be wasted on his apostles?

you do not think to be it, the Son of man is coming."—Matthew 24:36-44.

²¹ Does Jesus' illustration of the householder mean that, if he let us disciples of today know in advance the day and the hour of his coming for the settling of accounts, he would make sure of finding us all awake and on the watch? Hence ought we not to be given prior notice of the exact day and hour? That would be the way we do things today: give our receptionists advance notice in order that they may not be taken by surprise but have all things ready and not be embarrassed.

²² It is different with Jesus Christ, for his disciples are really his purchased slaves. At *all* times he desires them to be interested in his coming for judgment proceedings and so be serviceable at *all* times, out of love for him. He does not want them to be hypocritical eye-pleasers, putting on at the last minute before his arrival a show of being always active in his service. By not being notified ahead of time just exactly when he will arrive, the disciples have their love and obedience toward him tested constantly. Are they sincerely interested in his kingdom and are they *always* preparing for a share in that world government? Or, do they take time out to meddle in worldly affairs, say, in worldly politics? The King Jesus Christ detests lukewarm service, halfhearted attention. He wants no hypocrites in his kingdom.

²³ This vital point is emphasized by Jesus Christ in the illustrations of the "faithful and discreet

---

21. What questions and argument does Jesus' illustration raise?
22. Why does Jesus not give advance time notice of his coming?
23, 24. By what illustrations did Jesus emphasize the above point?

slave" and "that evil slave," the illustrations that he gave right after urging his disciples to 'prove themselves ready' at *all* times. (Matthew 24:45-51) There is a grand reward reserved for Christ's disciples who prove themselves to be faithful, discreet and loving slaves of his, uncompromisingly devoted to his handling of the promised world government. We are serving him not just for the sake of a reward. Nevertheless, he promises a grand reward out of his appreciation. Do we desire such a reward? It is the alternative of a punishment for unfaithfulness. (Luke 12:35-46) Out of love for Jehovah's anointed King we want the reward of faithfulness, do we not? Our answer being Yes! then let us do what the King Jesus Christ tells us:

²⁴ "What I say to you I say to all, Keep on the watch."—Mark 13:32-37; Luke 21:36.

²⁵ Let all of us watchers keep our eyes fixed on the "sign" that has been readable since 1914 C.E. (Matthew 24:3) May it stimulate us ever to keep alert, for the Messianic world government is imminent!

---

25. So, on what should we now keep our eyes fixed, and why?

CHAPTER 10

A "Great Crowd" Hails the Incoming World Government

ALL the nations of the earth, those inside the United Nations and those yet outside that world organization, are now gathered before God's enthroned King, his Son Jesus Christ. This is just as the Son of God foretold it when he was on earth nineteen centuries ago. In the closing illustration set out in his prophecy that details "the sign of [his] presence [*parousia*] and of the conclusion of the system of things," Jesus Christ said:

[2] "When the Son of man arrives in his glory, and all the angels with him, then he will sit down on his glorious throne. And all the nations will be gathered before him."—Matthew 25:31, 32.

[3] Many will contest the fulfillment of that inspired prophecy today, arguing that they do not see the more than four billion people of all nationalities, tribes and races gathered at some spacious place before a visible celestial throne with the Son of man, Jesus Christ, seated thereon, attended by "all the angels" of heaven. We agree with these objectors that they do not see such an

---

1, 2. Before whom are all earthly nations now gathered?
3. How may some argue in objecting to the foregoing statement?

international gathering. For one thing, how would all four billion inhabitants of earth get to such a gathering place, even if all the means of transportation that are available today were put at their disposal? Such a thing is out of the question, of course.

⁴ However, the human astronauts who made six landings on the moon in recent years were able to see the earthrise and the earthset from the moon's surface and also to see the entire revolving earthly globe as they traveled in their spacecraft between moon and earth. How much more so can the superhuman, glorified Jesus Christ take in the whole earthly scene from his throne far above the moon! Since his exaltation to his heavenly Father's right hand in 33 C.E., he has always been able to do this. So, then, in what sense is it that all the nations are gathered before him since his enthronement in heaven at the close of the Gentile Times in 1914?

⁵ Well, the situation has changed for the nations since their lease of world domination without interference by God's universal sovereignty ran out in 1914. (Luke 21:24; Psalm 110:1, 2) When Jesus Christ turned his attention to the nations from then on, he did so as reigning Messianic King. (Revelation 11:15; 12:10) He now faces them and inspects them as to their attitude regarding submission to the rightful Messianic rule. They are all treated as one worldwide political system, like a corporate group, and, together, they face him and deal with him over the paramount issue of world domination. They now have

4. Why does such a gathering raise no problem for Jesus now?
5. How have all nations been gathered before Christ enthroned?

to decide between national sovereignty and God's universal sovereignty by his Messianic kingdom. Because of the "authority of his Christ," God's enthroned Son is now authorized to "shepherd all the nations with an iron rod" and to dash them to pieces in due time. (Revelation 12:5; 19:15; Psalm 2:8, 9) The doomed nations have now gathered together under the United Nations organization, but not to yield to Christ's rule.

⁶ All the nations have been put on notice of the change in their position before Jehovah God the Appointer of the Gentile Times or "appointed times of the nations." (Daniel 4:16, 23, 25, 32; Luke 21:24) How so? By Jehovah's sending his Kingdom "ambassadors" to the nations, preaching 'this good news of the kingdom in all the inhabited earth for a witness to all the nations,' just as Jesus Christ foretold in Matthew 24:14. These Kingdom "ambassadors" are God's "chosen ones," the spiritual "brothers" of Jesus Christ. (2 Corinthians 5:20; Ephesians 6:20; John 20:17; Hebrews 2:11, 12) By such ambassadorial service and Kingdom proclamation to all the nations, they are gathered before God's anointed King, Jesus Christ, who holds the scepter of iron. Already Jehovah's Christian witnesses have introduced the Kingdom message into two hundred and ten lands, and as a result of this, disciples of the King Jesus Christ are found to be active in all those lands. (Matthew 28:19, 20) In this way all the nations have been gathered together before the enthroned King as notified ones, on a common footing, under like responsibility.—Compare Matthew 24:31; Isaiah 43:9.

---

6. How have all nations been notified of their changed position

DIVIDING KINGDOM SUPPORTERS
FROM NONSUPPORTERS

[7] How does "the Son of man" seated on his glorious heavenly throne deal with the nations thus gathered before him? In his illustration Jesus Christ goes on to say: "And he will separate people one from another, just as a shepherd separates the sheep from the goats. And he will put the sheep on his right hand, but the goats on his left."—Matthew 25:31-33.

[8] We should note that the King Jesus Christ does not separate the nations into two classes, one class against another class in political differences. Rather, he divides the *people* who live in those nations, thus allowing each person to make his own individual choice regardless of what the national government over him does. This separating work takes place during Christ's invisible "presence" in Kingdom power and great glory. (Matthew 24:3, 37, 39, 40) On what basis does this separating work take place? On the basis of their support of Christ's kingdom or their rejection of it. So, now, what kind of animal pictures the Kingdom supporters, and which kind the nonsupporters? Let us note:

[9] "Then the king will say to those on his right, Come, you who have been blessed by my Father, inherit the kingdom prepared for you from the founding of the world. For I became hungry and you gave me something to eat; I got thirsty and you gave me something to drink. I was a stranger

7, 8. (a) Does the King divide the nations as such according to political differences? (b) On what basis is the separation made?
9, 10. The sheeplike ones who are separated to the King's right did what?

and you received me hospitably; naked, and you clothed me. I fell sick and you looked after me. I was in prison and you came to me.' "—Matthew 25:34-36.

[10] Thus the "sheep" picture the supporters of the Messianic kingdom that was prepared for suchlike ones from the founding of the world of mankind. But since the King Jesus Christ has not been visible in the flesh during his current "presence" in Kingdom power and glory, how have these sheeplike individuals done such things to him? His illustration goes on to say:

[11] "Then the righteous ones will answer him with the words, 'Lord, when did we see you hungry and feed you, or thirsty, and give you something to drink? When did we see you a stranger and receive you hospitably, or naked, and clothe you? When did we see you sick or in prison and go to you?' And in reply the king will say to them, 'Truly I say to you, To the extent that you did it to one of the least of these my brothers, you did it to me.' "—Matthew 25:37-40.

[12] By the reference "my brothers," the King Jesus Christ means "his chosen ones," those who are "heirs indeed of God, but joint heirs with Christ." (Matthew 24:31; Romans 8:17) Of these spiritual brothers, there is yet a small remnant left on earth. All of these have been diligently engaged in fulfilling Jesus' prophecy, "This good news of the kingdom will be preached in all the inhabited earth for a witness to all the nations," for they know by the "sign" of Christ's invisible "presence"

11. How does the King answer the questions of the "sheep"?
12. How have the righteous "sheep" done these things, and why?

or *parousia* that the kingdom of God is near at the doors. For doing this since the close of the Gentile Times in 1914, they have been the ones who have experienced hunger, thirst, nakedness, sickness, absence from home or homelessness, and even imprisonment merely for preaching "this good news of the kingdom." (Matthew 24:14, 32, 33; Mark 13:9, 10; Luke 21:29-31) The "righteous" sheeplike ones come to the aid of the spiritual "brothers" of Christ because they are in favor of the Kingdom that these Christian "ambassadors" are preaching to them. They hail that kingdom as the rightful rulership for all mankind.

[13] They knowingly give aid for the furtherance of the Kingdom proclamation, because they pray for that world government and are in favor of it. That is why their aid to his spiritual "brothers" counts with the King Jesus Christ. They were long ago foreshadowed by the non-Jews who came to the aid of the imperiled Jews in the days of Queen Esther and Prime Minister Mordecai during the reign of Ahasuerus, emperor of Persia. —Esther 8:17; 9:3.

[14] Consequently, to these the King's promise applies: "Whoever gives you a cup of water to drink on the ground that you belong to Christ, I truly tell you, he will by no means lose his reward." (Mark 9:41) So now the righteous sheeplike relief-givers are rewarded with the privilege of joining the remnant of Christ's "brothers" in

---

13, 14. (a) Like what non-Jews in the days of Queen Esther have these "sheep" become? (b) They become the King's disciples, how?

preaching "this good news of the kingdom" world wide and sharing with the remnant in their sufferings for this cause. Actually they become "disciples" of Christ the King, making a dedication of themselves to the King's heavenly Father, Jehovah God, and getting baptized in water in symbol of such a dedication.—Matthew 28:19, 20.

¹⁵ For this dedicated course of action, the righteous sheeplike ones are made emissaries of God's Messianic kingdom, fully commissioned to preach this theocratic world government to persons of all tribes, nations, races and languages. Truly they become those "who have been blessed by [Christ's] Father."

¹⁶ For their faithfulness to the universal sovereignty of the King's Father they will be rewarded —not with an inheritance in the heavenly kingdom with Jesus Christ and his spiritual "brothers"— but with an inheritance in the earthly realm of the Messianic kingdom. The word "kingdom" is often used to mean the realm over which a kingdom rules. This Kingdom realm will be the earthly Paradise of which Jesus Christ spoke more than nineteen hundred years ago, shortly before his death on the stake, when he said to the dying sympathizer, "Truly I tell you today [Passover Day, 33 C.E.], You will be with me in Paradise." (Luke 23:43) But when God drove Adam and Eve out of the paradise in Eden, he had this restored Paradise in mind, according to what he said in Genesis 3:15, and that was at the "founding of the world."—Matthew 25:34.

---

15. The "sheep" are blessed with what commission of service?
16. How will the "sheep" inherit the Kingdom prepared long ago?

NONSUPPORTERS OF
THE INCOMING WORLD GOVERNMENT

[17] In contrast with the King's invitation to "inherit the kingdom [realm] prepared for [the righteous sheep] from the founding of the world," there is the judgment pronounced upon the symbolic "goats" of the illustration. Regarding these the parable goes on to say:

[18] "Then he will say, in turn, to those on his left, 'Be on your way from me, you who have been cursed, into the everlasting fire prepared for the Devil and his angels. For I became hungry, but you gave me nothing to eat, and I got thirsty, but you gave me nothing to drink. I was a stranger, but you did not receive me hospitably; naked, but you did not clothe me; sick and in prison, but you did not look after me.' Then they also will answer with the words, 'Lord, when did we see you hungry or thirsty or a stranger or naked or sick or in prison and did not minister to you?' Then he will answer them with the words, 'Truly I say to you, To the extent that you did not do it to one of these least ones, you did not do it to me.' "—Matthew 25:41-45.

[19] Here we might well ask, Does the King consider the matter as a mere unintentional oversight on the part of the "goat" class? Does he account their conduct as expressing merely ignorant neglect on their part? Certainly not, when we see that he calls these neglectful ones "cursed" and orders them to go off into the "everlasting fire prepared for the Devil and his angels." The King must rate or judge them as being wicked,

17, 18. What judgment is pronounced on the "goats," and why?
19. Does the King consider their conduct as ignorant neglect?

according to the Scriptural rule: "The curse of Jehovah is on the house of the wicked one, but the abiding place of the righteous ones he blesses." (Proverbs 3:33) But why should the "goat" class be cursed for mere failure to come to the aid and relief of Christ's "brothers"?

[20] If we say that the symbolic "goats" were "cursed" and condemned to destruction with the Devil and his angels merely for *ignorantly* neglecting Christ's "brothers," then, logically, we must argue that the symbolic "sheep" were blessed and rewarded with a place in the Kingdom realm merely for *ignorantly* doing good to Christ's "brothers." What real merit would there be, then, in the good that the "sheep" did to Christ's "brothers"? Or what demerit in the neglect that the "goats" did not realize that they were committing? Where, then, is the justice in rewarding the one ignorant class and punishing the other ignorant class? Justice is apparently nowhere in such treatment.

[21] Let us grant that both classes were ignorant of the rule that what they did or did not do to Christ's spiritual "brothers" they did or did not do to Christ himself. Still, they were not ignorant of the fact that they were dealing with his "brothers"! Why not?

[22] We have to take Jesus' parable of the sheep and the goats along with what he said earlier in his prophecy on "the sign of [his] presence and of the conclusion of the system of things." (Mat-

---

20, 21. If not knowing any rule, what did the "sheep" and "goats" know?
22. To whom were Christ's "brothers" to preach? With what reaction?

thew 24:3) He spoke of the approved work for his spiritual "brothers" when, at Matthew 24:14, he told them: "This good news of the kingdom will be preached in all the inhabited earth for a witness to all the nations." Not just to the so-called Christian nations or to Christendom, but to "all the nations" in "all the inhabited earth." Yet Jesus also told his spiritual "brothers": "Then people will deliver you up to tribulation and will kill you, and you will be objects of hatred by all the nations on account of my name."—Matthew 24:9.

[23] Hatred on account of his name means that Christ's "brothers" would identify themselves by their preaching of "this good news of the kingdom" world wide and by their making disciples for him, baptizing these. (Matthew 28:19, 20) In general, the people or the national governments that these people support refuse to acknowledge that these preachers of the Kingdom "good news" are Christ's spiritual "brothers." But does this really disprove that they are actually Christ's spiritual "brothers"? No!

[24] This general refusal of people to recognize Christ's spiritual "brothers" as being such, and this international hatred of them because of what they are preaching about the Kingdom have influenced people in their treatment of these. Where a nation has a Bill of Rights defending freedom of worship, individuals may not join in violently persecuting Christ's "brothers." But out of fear of public opinion or because of agreeing with it,

---

23. Does nonrecognition prove Christ's "brothers" not to be such?
24. When does neglect of Christ's "brothers" become inexcusable?

such abstainers from persecution refuse willfully to aid, relieve or support Christ's "brothers." So their negative attitude, their neglect, is not excusable.—Proverbs 29:18.

²⁵ Jesus' illustration of the sheep and the goats takes all of this into consideration. Failure to come to the aid and relief of Christ's "brothers" carries along with it a failure to aid and support Christ's kingdom, the incoming world government. This is a serious matter, and there is no middle ground, no compromise, no straddling of the fence, with respect to the issue of world government. Jesus Christ the King hates lukewarmness. (Revelation 3:16) Jesus also said: "He that is not on my side is against me, and he that does not gather with me scatters." (Matthew 12:30; Luke 11:23) On this basis there is no injustice on Jesus' part in declaring that the goatlike nonsupporters of his "throne" or kingdom are "cursed" and to be punished with the Devil and his angels. The title "Devil" means "Slanderer," and these "goats" are classed with the Chief Devil because they listen to the slanders of the Devil and his angels and are prejudiced against Christ's "brothers." (Revelation 12:10) They should share his fate.

²⁶ Let us, then, not be guilty of making excuses for the "goats" and thereby call into question the justice of Christ the King. Regardless of whether anyone likes the thought of it or not, Jesus' illustration closes with regard to the judgment executed on the faulty "goats" and the righteous "sheep," saying: "And these [symbolic goats]

25. Why can there be no indifference on the issue without punishment?
26. When will the King tell the "goats" to go off into the "fire"?

will depart into everlasting cutting-off, but the righteous ones into everlasting life." (Matthew 25:46) When will Christ the King tell these cursed "goats" to go off into the symbolic "fire," the "cutting-off" (Greek: ko'la·sis)? After the preaching of the Kingdom good news has been carried on earth wide by his spiritual "brothers" and "the end" comes on this system of things that is now in its "conclusion." (Matthew 24:3, 14) Then the "great tribulation" will break out world wide, but the "goats" will never survive it.—Matthew 24:21, 22.

[27] The everlasting "cutting-off" (ko'la·sis) of the "goats" is the opposite of the "everlasting life" with which the "sheep" are rewarded. It is an everlasting punishment, because this form of punishment will never be lifted from these "goats" who are executed in the "great tribulation." They will never have a resurrection from the dead. They suffer that other death that the Bible speaks of, "the second death," which is symbolized by "the lake of fire." They will no more be released from this symbolic "lake of fire" than Satan the Devil and his demon angels will. (Revelation 20:10-15; Genesis 3:15) They will perish in the "great tribulation" that will reach its peak in the "war of the great day of God the Almighty" at Har–Magedon.—Revelation 16:14, 16; 19:11-21.

THE SURVIVORS OF THE "GREAT TRIBULATION"

[28] We do not care to be 'cut off everlastingly' with the "goats" in the oncoming "great tribulation," do we? Not if we want to enjoy the in-

---

27. The "goats" have a "cutting-off" from what, for how long?
28, 29. The "sheep" survive what, as shown in Revelation 7: 13-15?

coming world government of Jehovah God by his Son Jesus Christ. Our sensible, God-honoring choice would be that of now proving ourselves to be like the blessed "sheep." The class made up of symbolic "sheep" will go alive through the "great tribulation." This survival leads on to their "everlasting life" under the incoming world government. There will be an unnumbered "great crowd" of such sheeplike survivors of the "great tribulation." We have assurance of this as stated in the dialogue between a special "elder" and one of Christ's "brothers," the apostle John. Concerning this dialogue we read:

29 "And in response one of the elders said to me: 'These who are dressed in the white robes, who are they and where did they come from?' So right away I said to him: 'My lord, you are the one that knows.' And he said to me: 'These are the ones that come out of the great tribulation, and they have washed their robes and made them white in the blood of the Lamb. That is why they are before the throne of God; and they are rendering him sacred service day and night in his temple; and the One seated on the throne will spread his tent over them.' "—Revelation 7:13-15.

30 God spreads his "tent" of protection over these white-robed persons. This explains how it is that, aside from the remnant of Christ's spiritual "brothers" to whom they have kept on doing good, they are the only ones out of all earth's population at the time that "come out of the great tribulation." During that "great tribu-

———
30. Under what protection do they survive, to stand before whom?

lation" all the thrones of the rulers of the nations have been overturned and destroyed. (Haggai 2:22) That is the reason why no other throne is spoken of in this particular vision of the apostle John but the "throne of God." (Revelation 7:10-15) No one else is seen seated on a throne but God. His position as Sovereign of the universe, including our earth, is vindicated!

[31] This vision shows that these white-robed survivors of the "great tribulation" have done more than what is illustrated in Jesus' parable of the sheep and the goats. They "have washed their robes and made them white in the blood of the Lamb." This stated fact emphasizes that they are believers in the Lamb of God, Jesus Christ, and have accepted his sin-atoning sacrifice, his shed blood. This is one of the factors that moves them to aid, relieve, and work with the Lamb's spiritual "brothers." Above all, they have looked to the Lamb's heavenly Father, the Universal Sovereign, for salvation out of the "great tribulation."

[32] The "great crowd" show that they meet the fundamental requirement for such salvation by the attitude they take toward God's throne and by what they publicly confess before it. This fact becomes plain to us as we read: "After these things [after the sealing of the 144,000 spiritual Israelites, the Lamb's spiritual brothers] I saw, and, look! a great crowd, which no man was able to number, out of all nations and tribes and peoples and tongues, standing before the throne and before the Lamb, dressed in white robes; and there were palm branches in their hands. And they keep on

31. What action, not shown in Jesus' parable, have they taken?
32. How do they meet the basic requirement for such salvation?

crying with a loud voice, saying: 'Salvation we owe to our God, who is seated on the throne, and to the Lamb.' "—Revelation 7:9, 10.

³³ In suitable dress, this "great crowd," which does not contain any spiritual Israelites, stands respectfully before God's throne, recognizing him as the World Ruler. (Revelation 11:15) As with palm branches, they unitedly hail Him as the Universal Sovereign, the One entitled to occupy a throne with universal governorship. (Compare John 12:12, 13.) They also acknowledge the "Chief Agent of life" whom Jehovah God has used, "the Lamb," Jesus Christ his Son. (Acts 3:15; John 1:29, 36) So they joyfully confess before heaven and earth the Source of their salvation out of the "great tribulation" and also his Chief Agent in that behalf.

³⁴ During this "conclusion of the system of things," notably since the year 1935 C.E., this "great crowd" has been assembled and unified despite national, racial and tribal extractions. They have heard the worldwide preaching of "this good news of the kingdom." Acting on the timely information published on page 250 (paragraph 34) of The Watchtower for August 15, 1934, they proceeded to dedicate themselves to Jehovah God through his Lamb Jesus Christ. Their dedication they symbolized by water baptism. They have joined the remnant of Christ's spiritual "brothers" in preaching the "good news" to the ends of the earth. How good it is to our ears to hear them thus hail Jehovah's incoming world government!

33. What acknowledgment do they make to God and his Son? How?
34. Since when, particularly, has there been a gathering of them?

CHAPTER 11

The Passing
of a Divided World

W E ARE now over nineteen centuries nearer to it. To what? To that beneficial world change that the Bible writer of the first century C.E. announced, saying: "The whole frame of this world is passing away." (1 Corinthians 7:31, *The New English Bible*) The "great crowd" of persons who are now preparing themselves for God's incoming world government rejoice that the passing away of the present divided world is imminent.—Revelation 7:9, 10.

[2] The United Nations organization, though now over thirty years old and having 147 member nations, has failed to heal the world's divided condition. Today many U.N. delegates realize that the most divisive force of all is worldly religion. Religious differences are deeply ingrained. Sects divide even the major religious systems. Christendom alone is split up a thousand ways or more. Despite their differences, God's Word lumps them all together as one world empire of false religion. It likens this religious empire to a woman, saying: "The woman whom you [the apostle John] saw means the great city that has a kingdom over the

_____

1. The "great crowd" rejoice over what imminent world change?
2, 3. (a) What has the United Nations failed to do for the world? (b) How does the Bible picture the divisive religious empire?

kings of the earth." (Revelation 17:18) Now, just who is this "woman" that is like an imperial city wielding influence over political rulers? The apostle John tells us, saying:

3 "Upon her forehead was written a name, a mystery: 'Babylon the Great, the mother of the harlots and of the disgusting things of the earth.' And I saw that the woman was drunk with the blood of the holy ones and with the blood of the witnesses of Jesus." (Revelation 17:5, 6) "The great harlot who sits on many waters, with whom the kings of the earth committed fornication, whereas those who inhabit the earth were made drunk with the wine of her fornication."—Revelation 17:1, 2.

4 The "kingdom" that Babylon the Great has had over the kings of the earth has been a harlotrous one, a course of religious "fornication." The people have suffered because of her mixing religion with politics. It has been a bitter potion for the common people to drink at her hand. It has made them reel as if drunk.

5 The mother "harlot" has spawned many other religious "harlots" and has made them members of her worldwide whorehouse. Today Babylon the Great hails the United Nations as she formerly did the League of Nations. She has put her trust in it instead of in God's Messianic kingdom, the incoming world government. So she rides upon it. For popularity's sake and for self-advantage she lets herself be carried along by it, thus to hold her religiously divided empire together in a sort of "unity with diversity." But the mount that she is riding is a dangerous one. Not without

4. How has her "fornication" affected the common people?
5. In what way does this harlot ride the "wild beast"? Why?

purpose does the Bible picture her mount as a scarlet-colored "wild beast" with seven heads and ten horns. This wild beast bears "blasphemous names." What Babylon the Great calls the beast is blasphemous to God.—Revelation 17:3.

⁶ How will God avenge the innocent blood with which she is "drunk"? By letting the "wild beast" organization turn upon her in hatred when He lets the "great tribulation" begin. Her destruction follows. (Revelation 17:15, 16; 19:1-3) Hence now, during this "conclusion of the system of things," Jehovah God has caused to be sounded out world wide the urgent cry: "Get out of her, my people, if you do not want to share with her in her sins, and if you do not want to receive part of her plagues. For her sins have massed together clear up to heaven, and God has called her acts of injustice to mind." (Revelation 18:4, 5) The remnant of Christ's spiritual "brothers" and also the "sheep" who make up the "great crowd" have obeyed God's command and gotten out. Consequently they will not perish with her in the "great tribulation."

AFTER "BABYLON THE GREAT" IS DESTROYED

⁷ After the empire of false religion is destroyed, there will be no Christendom to continue calling the United Nations organization "the political expression of the Kingdom of God on earth." The members of the U.N. and other nations not members of it will not think that they have done God a favor by destroying their former mistress who was drunk with the innocent blood of God's "holy ones" and of "the witnesses of Jesus." The nations

---

6. Who now get out of Babylon the Great, and why?
7. Does the "wild beast" mean to serve God by destroying her?

do not destroy the religious "harlot" purposely to avenge God and his persecuted people. They do it as an antireligious action, with no intention of making an exception of the true religion, "the form of worship that is clean and undefiled from the standpoint of our God and Father," as James 1:27 says. Already the more than half of the U.N. members that do not belong to Christendom disavow its being "the political expression of the Kingdom of God on earth."

8 So, after their destroying Babylon the Great (including Christendom), what will the nations adhering to or cooperating with the U.N. do? The same chapter that describes the "wild beast" organization as being like a seven-headed beast with ten horns tells us, saying: "These have one thought, and so they give their power and authority to the wild beast. These will battle with the Lamb, but, because he is Lord of lords and King of kings, the Lamb will conquer them. Also, those called and chosen and faithful with him will do so." (Revelation 17:13, 14) This battle will go on at the same time as what is described in Revelation 19:11-21. All of this is the "war of the great day of God the Almighty" at Har-Magedon.—Revelation 16:14, 16.

9 In this dramatic way the dream that the prophet Daniel interpreted to Nebuchadnezzar the king of ancient Babylon comes true. The kingdom that the God of heaven sets up in the days of the final rulers of the present political governments "will crush and put an end to all these kingdoms." (Daniel 2:44) This will be the all-time high point of the "time of distress such as has not been

8. After destroying Babylon the Great, what will the "beast" do?
9. What will befall those anti-Jehovah, anti-Christ "kings"?

made to occur since there came to be a nation until that time." (Daniel 12:1; Matthew 24:21, 22; Mark 13:19, 20) Concerning that time of universal war it is said to Jehovah's Field Marshal, Jesus Christ: "Jehovah himself at your right hand will certainly break kings to pieces on the day of his anger. He will execute judgment among the nations; he will cause a fullness of dead bodies. He will certainly break to pieces the head one over a populous land." (Psalm 110:5, 6) The "head one" of every "populous land" will lie crushed among a "fullness of dead bodies." Can we doubt it that this "day of his anger" will be a most turbulent time?

[10] The apostle Peter calls attention to the noisiness of that time of unparalleled world distress during which the long-established institutions of mankind undergo dissolution as if by the fire of a nuclear furnace. Writing, not to worldlings, but to Christians who may expect to witness these things and survive, Peter says: "Yet Jehovah's day will come as a thief, in which the heavens will pass away with a hissing noise, but the elements being intensely hot will be dissolved, and earth and the works in it will be discovered. Since all these things are thus to be dissolved, what sort of persons ought you to be in holy acts of conduct and deeds of godly devotion, awaiting and keeping close in mind the presence of the day of Jehovah, through which the heavens being on fire will be dissolved and the elements being intensely hot will melt! But there are new heavens and a new earth that we are awaiting according to his promise, and in these righteousness is to dwell."—2 Peter 3:10-13.

---

10. How does Peter describe the noisiness of Jehovah's "day"?

¹¹ Who is going to kindle that all-consuming fire that will rage all around this globe? Not the six or more nuclear-powered nations by the detonating of their overstock of bombs and missiles in surprise attacks on one another! No, but Jehovah God, the Creator of all the suns in all the galaxies of stars throughout the depths of space. The time of blazing conflagration will be "the day of Jehovah." Even though we Bible researchers know that we are living in the foretold "time of the end," the "conclusion of the system of things," yet that day for the removal of human rulerships will come as a thief. Man-made political governments, which have dominated mankind just as the literal heavens dominate the earth, will be unable to hold together but will disintegrate in chaotic disorganization. These symbolic "heavens" will, as the apostle Peter says, "pass away with a hissing noise." The prolonged sound, like that of escaping steam under pressure, may increase to a roaring as the governmental "heavens" crash in ruins.

¹² The heat of God's anger will be expressed so intensely against this ungodly system of things under Satan's control, that it will be liquefied, as it were, losing stability, internal cohesiveness. The "elements," that circumambient spirit that surrounds the earth and motivates earth's inhabitants in general, will lose whatever coolness and equanimity that it has had. Under the fiery indignation of Jehovah's day, that elemental spirit will get hot to white heat and will fire the people to wild acts of confused thinking, to violent, lawless fighting among themselves for self-survival.

11. Who will kindle the fire of that "day"? At what time?
12. In what sense will the "elements" melt on that "day"?

It will no longer hold the people together as a self-contained community. Thus the symbolic "elements" will dissolve, melt!

¹³ Well, then, could the "earth" that is to be destroyed mean our globe? No, it pictures human society according to the way it carries on under this system of things. Human society has many "works" to show for itself. It has many institutions, many organizations, many religious sects, many nationalistic ideals.

¹⁴ What will the "presence of the day of Jehovah" show all this form of human society and its selfish "works" to be? The "presence" of that fiery day of divine judgment will lay these things bare. They will be discovered in the condition in which they really are. The people will have these things made manifest to them as being condemned by the God of unselfishness and righteousness. As in the days of Noah before the global deluge, Jehovah will see "that the badness of man [is] abundant in the earth and every inclination of the thoughts of his heart [is] only bad all the time." (Genesis 6:5) So in line with his judgment of earthly matters, Jehovah will again wipe out a "world of ungodly people," the present human society that is symbolized by the expression "earth."—2 Peter 2:5; 3:7.

¹⁵ Those who have made themselves "no part of the world," namely, the remnant of Christ's spiritual "brothers" and the "great crowd" of Christ's "other sheep," will be caught in the midst of this fiery "day of Jehovah." What will they do in the midst of this "great tribulation" that will

---

13. What are the "earth and the works in it" here meant?
14. In what sense will "earth and the works in it" be discovered?
15. How will the remnant and the "great crowd" fare then?

have no repetition? (John 17:14, 16; 10:16) They
will not suffer dissolution along with the governmental "heavens," the temperamental "elements,"
and corrupt social "earth" and its worldly "works."
Under the "tent" of Jehovah's protection, they
will look out upon the stupendous things that are
taking place and will not be dismayed at the
violent passing of this divided world, the opposers
of Jehovah's sovereignty.—Psalm 37:34.

[16] These divinely protected ones will not be hor-
rified at the passing away of these old "heavens"
and old "earth." They will rejoice at this vindication of Jehovah's universal sovereignty. They will
become eyewitnesses of the "activities of Jehovah,
how he has set astonishing events on the earth."
They will realize that "he is making wars to cease
to the extremity of the earth." (Psalm 46:8, 9)
They will look forward to the establishing of "new
heavens and a new earth," which they have so
long awaited with endurance. Elatedly they will
rejoice that at last the time has actually arrived
for Jehovah God to fulfill his promise of "new
heavens and a new earth." (2 Peter 3:13) O what
a now indescribable experience it will be for them
to survive the "great tribulation" and its "war of
the great day of God the Almighty" at Har–
Magedon and be preserved alive into His New
Order!

16. These become what kind of eyewitnesses of God's activities?

CHAPTER 12

How We Can Enjoy the World Government Forever

WORLD GOVERNMENT by the Creator of heaven and earth will be a thing to enjoy forever. It will stand for all time and will ever handle mankind's affairs with perfect success. After the storm clouds of mankind's greatest "time of distress" have passed over, this world government of Jehovah God by Jesus Christ will be the "new heavens" that will arch out brilliantly over all the earth. On earth a new and righteous human society will spring up that will respond harmoniously to the governmental "new heavens." The way to Paradise will be opened!

² Just think of it: There are to be direct eyewitnesses of the setting up of the "new heavens" in which righteousness is to dwell. Will these eyewitnesses include us? We can rightly ask ourselves that question, for the Bible assures us that there will be survivors without specified number who will be here on earth to hail with joy the inauguration of the "new heavens." By no means will those "new heavens" be established over a depopulated earth. Right from the start of their righteous rule they will have willing subjects here

1. Under the "new heavens" what will spring up on earth?
2. What question may we ask ourselves about being eyewitnesses?

on the cleansed earth. By the unmerited kindness of the Creator of the "new heavens and a new earth," the remnant of Christ's spiritual "brothers" and the unnumbered "great crowd" of those who aided and supported Christ's "brothers" will have an experience like that of the apostle John. Their eyes will be entranced, as were John's, at the vision about which he said: "And I saw a new heaven and a new earth; for the former heaven and the former earth had passed away, and the sea is no more."—Revelation 21:1; Isaiah 65:17.

³ What? Will the seven seas of our globe be evaporated during the fiery "day of Jehovah" and be no more? Happily not! John speaks of a symbolic "sea." Consequently, when, in due time, the remnant and the "great crowd" of their fellow survivors look out over the new scene, they will not see on the cleansed earth anywhere any restless, dissatisfied, turbulent society expressing opposition to God's established world government. The "world of ungodly people" will have been dried up, wiped out, removed during the "great tribulation" that will have just ended. Such a "sea" of polluted, filth-laden water will not survive the judgment day on which Jehovah's anger is poured out like fire.—Revelation 8:8, 9; 10:2; 13:1; 16:3; 17:15; 2 Peter 2:5; Isaiah 17:12; 57:20.

⁴ That boisterous element on earth that has roared against God's world government by Christ will not be the only opposition group that will be put out of action. Another opposition group,

---

3. In what way will it be that "the sea is no more"?
4. What other element is to be removed besides the "sea"?

an even more powerful one, will be removed from the neighborhood of our earth. Who are these latter ones? The symbolic Dragon, Satan the Devil, and all his demon angels. After the war in heaven that followed upon the birth of God's Messianic kingdom at the close of the Gentile Times in 1914, that "ruler of the demons," together with his legions of demon angels, was ousted from heaven. Down to the vicinity of our earth they were hurled, to be restrained there for "a short period of time." In great anger over his ouster and eternal debarment from heaven, this superhuman Dragon, like a huge Leviathan, has churned up the "sea" of restless humanity against the newborn kingdom of God by Christ and its reign of a thousand years.—Revelation 12:3-13; Job 41:1-32.

[5] After the Dragon, Satan the Devil, sees his earthly servants defeated in the "war of the great day of God the Almighty" at Har–Magedon, he and his invisible legions reach the end of their "short period of time." What then? In a prophetic preview of the postwar period, the apostle John saw all that demon band removed from the neighborhood of our earth and imprisoned, chained, in an abyss, under a seal that was not to be broken for a thousand years. In this thoroughgoing way both heaven and earth are cleared of all wicked opposers of Jehovah's world government by his Christ. (Revelation 16:14, 16; 19:19 through 20:3) What an ideal condition now prevails universally! How enjoyable life will become for us

---

5, 6. (a) When and how will Satan and the demon angels be put to silence? (b) In support of what will the "great crowd" cry out?

if we prove worthy to be part of the "great crowd" of "tribulation" survivors! Satan the Devil and all who imitate him in challenging God's rightful sovereignty of heaven and earth will have been silenced and removed. In hearty support of Jehovah's sovereignty the "great crowd" will take their stand before his throne and cry out:

[6] "Salvation we owe to our God, who is seated on the throne, and to the Lamb."—Revelation 7:9, 10, 14, 15.

A LIFE-GIVING WORLD GOVERNMENT

[7] Salvation out of the "great tribulation" is one thing, of surpassing grandeur indeed, but eternal life in good health and happiness is another thing, of all-transcending grandeur. This latter benefit is what the divine world government will offer to earth's inhabitants. In words of sheer beauty, the apostle John tells us of this. After remarking that then "the sea is no more," he says, "I saw also the holy city, New Jerusalem, coming down out of heaven from God and prepared as a bride adorned for her husband. With that I heard a loud voice from the throne [hence God's voice] say: 'Look! The tent of God [not, the throne of God] is with mankind, and he will reside with them, and they will be his peoples. And God himself will be with them. And he will wipe out every tear from their eyes, and death will be no more, neither will mourning nor outcry nor pain be anymore. The former things [including the former heaven and earth] have passed

---

7. Revelation 21:2-5 shows that God's government gives mankind what?

away.' And the One seated on the throne [God] said: 'Look! I am making all things new.'"
—Revelation 21:2-5.

⁸ The expression, "the holy city, New Jerusalem," denotes a government, just as ancient Jerusalem in the days of King David and his son, King Solomon, denoted a government, these kings being said to sit on "Jehovah's throne" as His representatives. (1 Chronicles 29:23) Has any government till now been able to give to the people on earth what the New Jerusalem will bring, wiping away of tears because of calamities and heartaches, removal of death, mourning, outcry and pain of heart? All mankind's mournful condition till now answers No! But the New Jerusalem can and will bring those blessings because it is a government from God. God's beloved Son, Jesus Christ, tasted a sacrificial human death for all mankind to lift inherited death from us forever. For the realization of that he must reign for a thousand years.—1 Timothy 2:5, 6; Hebrews 2:9; 1 Corinthians 15:24-27.

⁹ A government is not an automaton, a thing set in motion and running automatically. To function, it requires governors or officials. Who, then, will compose the God-given New Jerusalem? God's angel explained to the apostle John that the New Jerusalem is "the bride, the Lamb's wife." That signifies that it is the congregation of the 144,000 disciples and joint heirs with Jesus Christ the Lamb, all spiritual Israelites. (Revelation 21:9-14; 7:4-8; 14:1-4; 19:7, 8; 2 Corin-

8. The New Jerusalem represents what and brings what to men?
9. The New Jerusalem will consist of what?

thians 11:2) However, because the New Jerusalem class is spoken of as a bride, a wife, this class is not here spoken of as reigning, but it is her Bridegroom that reigns.

¹⁰ Just as "Jehovah's throne" was located in ancient earthly Jerusalem and King David and his succession of kings sat upon that throne as Jehovah's visible representatives, so the case is similar here with the New Jerusalem. We read: "The throne of God and of the Lamb will be in the city." It is from this throne that the "river of water of life" flows for the eternal life of the subjects of God's kingdom by Christ. (Revelation 22:1, 3) Accordingly, in the New Jerusalem the Lamb Jesus Christ sits upon "Jehovah's throne" as the Messianic King anointed by Him. This royal descendant of Kings David and Solomon is greater than these forefathers of his, for his kingdom is heavenly and will be a world government: "He will have subjects from sea to sea and from the River [Euphrates] to the ends of the earth." (Psalm 72:8) His rulership will be global.—Zechariah 9:9, 10; Psalm 110:1, 2.

¹¹ At a time not indicated, the remnant of Christ's joint heirs will pass off the earthly scene and, by means of the "first resurrection," they will be united with their heavenly Bridegroom and thus the entire Bride class of 144,000 joint heirs will be completed. (Revelation 20:4, 6) But the "great crowd" of their virginlike companions

10. In what way do God and Jesus occupy the throne in "the city"?
11. (a) When and how is the Bride class completed? (b) What does the World Ruler, Jesus, become to his subjects, and on what basis?

will continue here on earth as subjects of the
World Governor, Jesus Christ. (Psalm 45:14)
Though being a world ruler, he will be a father
to them. To his faithful subjects he will become
their Eternal Father, for he died for them all
that he might be their Life-Giver. As "the last
Adam," he was made "a life-giving spirit" in
their behalf.—1 Corinthians 15:45; Isaiah 9:6.

12 It is said of the "great crowd" that "they have
washed their robes and made them white in the
blood of the Lamb." This sacrificial "Lamb of
God" therefore acts as God's High Priest at His
spiritual temple. Logically, then, what is the first
thing that the "great crowd" of 'white-robed'
ones do after they "come out of the great tribulation"? Like Noah and his family right after
the Deluge, the "great crowd" address themselves
to Jehovah's worship. "That is why they are before the throne of God; and they are rendering
him sacred service day and night in his temple."
(Revelation 7:9, 10, 14, 15; John 1:29, 36) They
know that, under God's world government by
Christ, no form of worship will ever be permitted
but the one true religion, the pure worship of
the one living and true God, Jehovah. This will
be the one and only religion of the "new earth."
It will be a unifying source for all.

13 Will the surviving "great crowd" be the only
ones used to transform our earthly globe into a
surpassingly beautiful Paradise? No, but the re-
deemed human dead, after their resurrection, will
share in this delightful work. This will include the

12. To what will the "great crowd" apply themselves? Where?
13. Who on earth will share in making all earth a Paradise?

sympathetic man who died at Jesus' side.—Luke 23:43.

¹⁴ The "keys of death and of Ha'des [the common grave of mankind]" are to be used. Jesus Christ has them since his own resurrection. O joy, he will use them for the resurrecting of all those to whom his ransom sacrifice applies! The works that these resurrected ones do during his thousand-year reign will be the basis for their being judged. Those proving willfully disobedient and irreformable will forfeit all claim on life. They will get the penalty of a death from which there will be no resurrection.—Revelation 1:18; 20:11-15; Acts 24:15; John 5:28, 29.

¹⁵ The cleansing of the universe will be capped finally by the destruction of Satan the Devil and his demons, the promoters of wickedness. (Revelation 20:7-10; Genesis 3:15) What a blessing to our earth! Beautifying it then will be one world under one government in loving loyalty to God's rightful sovereignty.

¹⁶ O what a blessed prospect is before us in the light of God's Word! Irresistibly it tugs at our heartstrings. O, then, with open arms we bid you welcome, you long-awaited world government. The "sign" of your imminence has appeared before our eyes and ever becomes more meaningful. Clearly within our reach is the loving provision for us to enjoy eternal life on a Paradise earth under your rightful rulership. Our hearts, burning with appreciation, move us to embrace such a precious opportunity.

---

14. Who will use the "keys of death and of Ha'des"? For whom?
15. How will the cleansing of the universe be capped?
16, 17. Appreciation of God's undeserved kindness moves us to do what?

[17] Thanks to your Creator, Jehovah, the Maker of heaven and earth, we know now what to do in this "year of goodwill on the part of Jehovah." (Isaiah 61:2; 49:8; 2 Corinthians 6:1, 2) The privilege is ours to become the dedicated, baptized disciples of Jehovah's Chief Agent for blessing mankind. (Matthew 28:19, 20) In his footsteps we will press forward, joyfully proclaiming everywhere "this good news of the kingdom," until all enemies bow to your glorious triumph, O you our incoming world government, God's kingdom.

GOOD NEWS
—TO MAKE YOU HAPPY

You will find this good news in the book with the above title. It tells how you can enjoy total happiness right here on earth—forever. As it shows, this certain prospect is held forth in the Bible.

The 192-page book **Good News—to Make You Happy** is only 25 cents (U.S.) a copy, postpaid. Write to **Watchtower**, using an address below.

ALASKA 99507: 2552 East 48th Ave., Anchorage. **AUSTRALIA:** 11 Beresford Road, Strathfield, N.S.W. 2135. **BAHAMAS:** Box N-1247, Nassau, N.P. **BARBADOS:** Fontabelle Rd., Bridgetown. **BELIZE:** Box 257, Belize City. **BRAZIL:** Rua Guaíra, 216, Bosque da Saúde, 04142 São Paulo, SP; Caixa Postal 12.896, 01000 São Paulo, SP. **CANADA M6A 1Z5:** 150 Bridgeland Ave., Toronto, Ont. **ENGLAND:** Watch Tower House, The Ridgeway, London NW7 1RN. **FIJI:** Box 23, Suva. **FRANCE:** 81 rue du Point-du-Jour, 92100 Boulogne-Billancourt. **GERMANY, FEDERAL REPUBLIC OF:** Postfach 5920, D-6200 Wiesbaden 1. **GHANA:** Box 760, Accra. **GUYANA:** 50 Brickdam, Georgetown 16. **HAWAII 96814:** 1228 Pensacola St., Honolulu. **HONG KONG:** 312 Prince Edward Rd., Second Floor, Kowloon. **INDIA:** South Avenue, Santa Cruz, Bombay 400054. **IRELAND:** 86 Lindsay Rd., Glasnevin, Dublin 9. **JAMAICA:** 41 Trafalgar Rd., Kingston 10. **KENYA:** Box 47788, Nairobi. **LEEWARD ISLANDS:** Box 119, St. Johns, Antigua. **LIBERIA:** P.O. Box 171, Monrovia. **MALAYSIA:** 20 Scotland Close, Penang. **NEWFOUNDLAND, CANADA A1C 2M1:** 239 Pennywell Rd., St. John's. **NEW ZEALAND:** 6-A Western Springs Rd., Auckland 3. **NIGERIA:** P.O. Box 194, Yaba, Lagos State. **PAKISTAN:** 8-E Habibullah Rd., Lahore 3. **PANAMA:** Apartado 1386, Panama 1. **PAPUA NEW GUINEA:** Box 113, Port Moresby. **PHILIPPINES, REPUBLIC OF:** P.O. Box 2044, Manila 2800; 186 Roosevelt Ave., San Francisco del Monte, Quezon City 3010. **PORTUGAL:** Apartado 21.022, Lisbon 2. **RHODESIA:** 35 Fife Avenue, Salisbury. **SIERRA LEONE:** Box 136, Freetown. **SOUTH AFRICA:** Private Bag 2, P.O. Elandsfontein, 1406. **SRI LANKA, REP. OF:** 62 Layard's Road, Colombo 5. **SWITZERLAND:** Ulmenweg 45; P.O. Box 477, CH-3601 Thun. **TRINIDAD:** 2 La Seiva Road, Maraval, Port of Spain. **UNITED STATES OF AMERICA:** 117 Adams St., Brooklyn, N.Y. 11201.